Praise for previous work b

'Your book is the best text I have read on the subject.'

JC, Leicester

'...thank you for such a superbly readable, interesting and informative book...'

JE, Kent

'Your book was able to guide me through all aspects of the business in an achievable and sensible way. I felt extremely motivated after reading it and know that it will act as a permanent guide throughout my MLM career and also for the people I sponsor.'

MG, Manchester

'...the most positive source of research I have come across and makes a pleasant change from sceptical and misinformed newspaper columnists.'

ML, Birmingham

'Your book was an inspiration, thank you.'

AM, Wales

'...I was most impressed. You cut through the hype and get to the facts in a most objective manner.'

RW, Hampshire

'Reading your book was the best thing I've done since I started in MLM as I found it very positive, informative and encouraging. It answered many of the questions which have been going around in my head. I have finally found the importance of reading good books in order to help me build my business and, of course, my dreams.'

JM, Ireland

'Thank you for introducing me to a new future through your book.'

JRC, Cornwall

'I found your book very interesting and inspirational.'

MM, Malta

'I have read your book from cover to cover over the past three days and I would like to thank you very much for providing such a wealth of information regarding MLM and also for providing such an entertaining read.'

KR, Avon

'Thank you for the clear and straightforward illustration of MLM. I see it as a good opportunity to improve my income and help others do the same.'

BK, Uganda

'Your excellent book is a great asset...'

GR Australia

Network Marketing:
How To Make It Pay

Also by Peter Clothier:

Multi-Level Marketing:
A Practical Guide To Successful Network Selling

Second Edition (Kogan Page)

Network Marketing:
How To Make It Pay

Peter Clothier
&
Trevor Lowe

Insight Network Marketing Library

Network Marketing: How To Make It Pay
Peter Clothier & Trevor Lowe

Insight Publishing Ltd
Serendipity House
Greytree Road
Ross-on-Wye
Herefordshire HR9 7DQ
Phone: 01989-564496
Fax: 01989-565596

First published 1995
© Peter Clothier 1995

Notice of Liability
While great care has been taken in the preparation of this
publication, it should not be used as a substitute for appropriate
professional advice. Neither the authors nor Insight Publishing
can accept any liability for loss or damage occasioned by any
person acting as a result of the material in this book.

ISBN: 1-899298-01-0

Cover design by Just Proportion, Louth, Lincolnshire
Printed and bound in Great Britain by Biddles Ltd, Guildford,
Surrey

This book is dedicated
to those who have a dream
and recognise
that it will only become a reality
through their own efforts.

Acknowledgements

Special thanks to Debbie Clothier and David Barber for their generous help in the preparation of this book.

Contents

Introduction

In the space of thirteen years Trevor Lowe and his wife Jackie have built a network marketing business which at the time of writing has a turnover of more than £10,000,000 a year through a network of over 20,000 independent distributors. Both these figures are increasing daily. Their income from this business is equivalent to a few per cent of its turnover, a figure you can calculate for yourself, yet this is only their UK business! In virtually every country in which their company operates there are many distributors who have Trevor and Jackie somewhere 'upline' from them. The sales of all these distributors around the world provide additional income for Trevor and Jackie. Every day the number of distributors within their network increases. Every year the average turnover per distributor increases. This incredible business was started with a financial investment of about fifteen pounds. They made no capital investments, nor did they borrow. No office was rented, no staff were employed. Every distributor within their network operates a wholly independent business with no contractual link to the Lowes or any other distributor. This is a business opportunity well worth further investigation!

I'm Peter Clothier, co-author of this book and author of *Multi-level Marketing – A Practical Guide to Successful Network Selling* (Kogan Page, 1992, now in its 2nd edition). Aside from writing I also work with my wife Debbie in her very successful network business.

Both Trevor and I feel strongly that there is room for a book that tells prospective, new and aspiring networkers some more truths about network marketing – information which we think is essential to absorb at an early stage if long-term success is desired. One truth is that you can become a millionaire through network marketing. Another truth is that few people do, and one of the reasons is that they are unprepared for the realities of the business. There are few books on this subject. Most give a good outline of what the business concept is all about, and good advice on how to build a network. What they don't tell you is what really happens when you start building this type of business in earnest.

- Does it really only cost £75 or less to start in network marketing?
- Can I really build a business in eight hours a week?
- How do I find 500 distributors?
- How many people do I need to know?
- How fast will my income increase?
- Will my expenses be high?
- Does my attitude really make such a difference?
- What questions will people ask, and how do I answer them?
- How can I approach people really effectively?
- What is it that people who have made £1,000,000 in network marketing are doing differently from those who fail to reach their goals?

The answers to these and many other questions will be revealed in depth within this book.

Trevor and I have spent many hours discussing the content and what you will read is the result of a great deal of collaboration. We think you will find this book to be a breath of fresh air in the field of network marketing literature. It will tell you many things that new distributors are not often made aware of when they start in network marketing. If more people were told these things there would be a smaller drop-out rate amongst distributors of all network marketing companies, and perhaps more people would go on to earn £1,000,000.

This book is not a network marketing primer, it assumes a working knowledge of the basic concepts involved. It is not a comprehensive guide to everything you will ever need to know about the business. We do not profess to have all the 'right' answers, and some networkers might disagree with many of the opinions and conclusions offered. The purpose of this book is to help you to make a lasting success of your network marketing business by making sure that you understand some of the most important facts and principles involved, as we have identified them through practical experience and observation.

Chapter 1

How this book will help you make £1,000,000 in 5 –10 years

Trevor and Jackie Lowe earned their first £1,000,000 from network marketing within ten years. As you will see from the figures in this book, my wife and I, too, are on target to earn £1,000,000 before our network marketing business is ten years old.

A million pounds sounds like a great deal of money, more than most people get their hands on within their lifetime. But put it into perspective; how much money might a person on an average income earn during their working life of say, 40 years. Ignoring inflation, the starting salary might be £10,000 p.a., rising with experience and promotions to perhaps £25,000 p.a. by retirement age. That is a total of around £750,000 in 40 years. Obviously many people have less well paid jobs, but many have much better ones. So it is not too difficult or unusual for someone in a reasonable job or business to earn themselves £1,000,000 within 40 years.

Can you really speed up the earning process by a factor of four or five? We would not have written this book if we did not think it was well within your reach to do so. The technique is simple and relies on two concepts:

- *You* have to find some extra hours a week and be prepared to work consistently for as long as it takes, namely five to ten years;
- *We* will show you how to maximise and multiply that time so that you can build yourself a business that will provide you with the promised income within the stated timescale.

But first you have to choose a suitable network marketing company – one which is likely to have long-term prospects. (This could be your most difficult task. If you have not already made a decision, the information in this book will help you.) Your chosen company must provide a product range you can identify with and be enthusiastic about recommending and selling.

Then, by following the advice in this book, and of course the advice of your upline and company, there is no reason why you could not make an overall profit of at least £5,000 in your first twelve months.

In your second year you will continue to develop your network business, no doubt more effectively with the benefit of experience. A conservative estimate is that your income will double.

This should be repeated for several more years (it will not double indefinitely – but your income will continue to increase substantially each year), and at the end of, say, the eighth year your accumulated income will almost certainly be in excess of £1,000,000.

You might have gone full-time by then, but not necessarily. You might work more slowly than this. Suppose it took you two years to make your first £5,000. This would simply put you back one year – it would take you nine years to reach the quoted figure.

On the other hand, what if you work a lot faster and more effectively than most? For example, I know someone who made £30,000 in his first year and doubled it in the second. He'll take only five years to reach his £1,000,000!

Action agenda

1. Start believing that you can make £1,000,000 in this business.

2. To do so, prepare yourself for at least five years' consistent effort.

3. Check your progress by keeping this record of your income from your network marketing business:

	Best Bonus Payment	Accumulated Income
After 1 year		
After 2 years		
After 3 years		
After 4 years		
After 5 years		

Chapter 2

An introduction to network marketing

Before we get into our discussion about network marketing we should make sure that both readers and writers are on the same wavelength about the meaning of the term. The contents of this book refer only to what we consider to be *genuine* network marketing, that is a business opportunity with at least these three characteristics:

- Backed and administered by a substantial and stable company with effective and experienced management;
- Offering quality products easy to sell regularly to consumers outside the network at a price which provides a reasonable profit for the seller;
- Paying bonuses and commissions which are based solely upon product sales.

We believe these to be the minimum necessary to ensure that a long-term, profitable and secure business can be confidently developed.

Every month a large number of schemes come into existence which use variations and corruptions of the network marketing concept. Every month an almost equally large number of these schemes go out of existence. In most cases hundreds, if not thousands, of people lose a small or large sum of money which had been 'invested' under the impression that big money would be quickly accumulated. A few people will have made a large profit at the expense of the majority.

Many of the promoters of these schemes describe them as network marketing opportunities, so many of the disgruntled losers (and therefore all their friends) develop a distaste for anything bearing the same name. This may be irrational – we have all heard about fraudulent banks, pension schemes, financial advisors, but we all use genuine ones – however, it is a fact of life. So please remember that we are discussing only genuine network marketing opportunities throughout this book.

What is network marketing?

You might be very new to this form of business, so it is a good idea to re-establish what it actually is. Network marketing is just one way for a manufacturer or supplier to reach consumers of its products or services. Instead of using high street shops, national advertising, direct mail and any number of other marketing methods, the company offers to individuals like you and me the opportunity to sell its products. In order to recruit enough 'independent distributors' to build the turnover to worthwhile levels the company devises a commission structure which rewards every distributor for selling products and for finding and training new distributors to do the same.

The details of the commission structures (usually called sales and marketing plans) vary greatly from company to company but the principles remain the same. A typical plan might pay out around 50% of the retail price in commissions and bonuses. Perhaps half of this will go to the person who makes the sale. The rest is split into smaller amounts which are paid to various distributors 'upline', if they have qualified for bonus payments under the relevant criteria in the marketing plan.

The result of all this is that a very attractive business opportunity is available to distributors who duplicate their efforts by finding and teaching others to sell, recruit and teach. At the same time, the originating company is effectively increasing its turnover at possibly less cost than other more traditional methods of marketing.

The advantages

It is important that we are clear about the special advantages offered by a network marketing business. It is unlikely that you would experience all these benefits together in any other single business. We should also make clear now that throughout this book we are concerned with the businesses carried on by the independent distributors (sole proprietors or partnerships) who sell the products and recruit new distributors on behalf of the network marketing company. The running of the company itself is not the concern of this book.

- *Start-up:* Initial costs are negligible compared to most businesses, with no capital expenditure required. You will not need to spend more than £100 on a business starter kit and registration fee, and possibly not much more on product samples (depending on the type of product). Break-even can be achieved within days, or even hours.

- *Potential:* Income potential is considerably higher than most businesses due to the nature of the network marketing concept. (This is explained in more detail later in this book.)

- *Risk:* Virtually no financial risks need be taken. No major changes in existing business or employment obligations are necessary. Late payers and bad debts are rare as customers usually pay at the time of ordering.

- *Simplicity:* This is a ready-made business, with no premises to acquire, no staff to employ, no stock or equipment to purchase, and no special skills needed. Profit on personal sales is usually immediate, and all other income arrives in the form of a single, punctual, monthly bonus cheque.

- *Flexibility:* Hours of work are completely flexible. The business can be worked satisfactorily part-time as a source of additional income, or built to substantial income levels in a reasonably short period with full-time input.

- *Expansion:* Procedures for national expansion (and international, where the company offers this opportunity) are simple and straightforward.

- *Training:* Formal and on-the-job training is provided by the company and upline, and is usually comprehensive, regular and free (or inexpensive). Close personal support in all business activities should be given by committed sponsors.

- *Competition:* This is generally not an issue in network marketing due to the small number of customers (compared with traditional retailing) serviced by each individual distributor. Contrary to popular opinion, nor is 'saturation' an issue.

- *Equal opportunity:* There are no selection procedures, other than payment of an initial fee and willingness to abide by a standard contract. No previous experience is necessary and the same opportunity is available to all. Basic social skills and the necessary desire and determination are the only prerequisites for success.

What they say...

Here are comments from a random selection of people in network marketing, explaining what they find so appealing about their businesses. Some are new to the business, others are very experienced; some have created new wealth, others do it for a little extra spending money; some are male, some female. They are all different, and several different companies are represented.

'It's not work, I enjoy it too much! I've made more friends in the last two years than in the previous ten. We just keep on doing the same things and the business keeps on growing. Financial independence is now just a matter of time.'

'I just love the freedom it gives me. The business has opened up many new directions and positive changes in my life through all the new people I've met.'

'We were living from month to month, with no savings, just bills, just broke. In network marketing we saw hope, a means of getting out of debt and a chance to expand our lifestyle. Our dreams have

become much larger as we have realised the true earning potential.'

'We never dreamed we could alter our lifestyle so much in such a short time. In our first year we earned £40,000. This second year we are on track to earn over £80,000. Where else can you go for a £45 start-up and get those kind of results in just two years?'

'I investigated the business opportunity and discovered I could do something I really enjoyed AND make money at the same time. The most rewarding part is meeting new people and making new friends.'

'I needed a job where I could dictate my own hours and build a business around my children. I started to help pay for school fees but my earnings have now gone way beyond that.'

'By the time I was 32 my wife and I had built a construction company with 30 employees and a £1,000,000 turnover. The future looked rosy until the recession took its toll and wiped up out. Now, with our network marketing business, we know that with sustained effort we can rebuild the lifestyle we had... and more... by doing something we are proud of and enjoy.'

'I was working as a computer technician when a cousin introduced me to network marketing. What impressed me was that I could remember when my cousin had been broke. When I saw how successful he had become with network marketing I figured I could do something with it too. I worked hard and *after four months I was able to go full-time. I've been happy ever since!'*

Action agenda

1. Make absolutely sure you are involved with genuine network marketing; Chapters 2 and 9 will help you.

2. Why do you want to start a network marketing business?

   ....
   ....
   ....
   ....

   Signed ....
   Date ....

   You should regularly pick up this book and look at what you have written here, especially when you feel disheartened. So make it a good (and true) reason!

3. Make some plans. With the help of your sponsor, write down what you will achieve, and the income level needed to achieve it, by the time you have been building your business for:

   2 years ....
   ....
   ....
   5 years ....
   ....
   ....

10 years ....
....
....

Commit yourself!

Chapter 3

The key to security, profitability and growth

If you are going to achieve your £1,000,000 income in the most efficient way, you should not treat your network marketing business like any other business you may have been involved in.

One of the most important things to understand in order to succeed in network marketing is how different it is to conventional ways of doing business. The enormous turnover of the Lowes' network has been achieved without the help of retail shops or advertising, and with only a small amount of specific sales activity by any particular person. How is this possible? It is only possible by network marketing – building a large network of independent distributors.

What makes this business so different is that massive product movement, and hence cash turnover, is actually achieved by most distributors *not* spending the majority of their time concentrating on selling. The main thrust of their efforts is directed towards building their own networks. Compare this with virtually any other type of business where the major portion of effort must go towards making the sale. Network marketing focuses on *people* more than *sales*. This is precisely the reason why network marketing can offer the unique benefits we have mentioned to so many more people than traditional businesses. This book will show you exactly how such large product volumes can be achieved by concentrating on people rather than sales.

Do not assume that this approach ignores the vital importance of product sales. Sales *must* be made by every active distributor on a regular and consistent basis, otherwise there is no point at all in building a network. Indeed, a good network marketing company will require a minimum personal retail turnover as part of the qualification to receive certain bonuses.

The network building process

All businesses become successful by supplying desirable products or services to as many buyers as possible. Traditionally this may be done by such expensive methods as developing a nationwide chain of retail stores over a number of years and maximising the turnover of each one by regular mass media advertising. Alternatively a company may concentrate its efforts on mail order by the production and mailing of many thousands of catalogues with a view to a large number of small sales. This is again a very expensive method of reaching a lot of people.

Network marketing companies take a different view. They say, in effect: 'Why don't *you* help us find those thousands of small-scale retail outlets (i.e. independent distributors)? Build us a network of people through whom we can reach a large number of customers and in return we'll give you a percentage of the resulting turnover instead of spending it on traditional marketing activities.'

The sales of active individual distributors might range from, say, four to forty orders per month, which is a negligible figure in comparison with the amount required for the successful running of the network marketing company itself. To prosper the company must promote, through its distributors, the building of a large network, large enough so that all those small individual orders add up to a substantial turnover.

In this respect, your own network business is in much the same position. If you want a substantial business you will not do it with a dozen people each turning over a small amount per month. Nor will you do it with dozen people turning over a large amount per month. You are going to have to involve hundreds and eventually thousands of people.

This may seem like a formidable task but like any major achievement it is done over a period, one step at a time. The first step which your sponsor will recommend is to begin the process of developing your network by identifying some of the people who might like to be part of it. The hub of your network marketing business, around which your success revolves, is presenting the business opportunity and the products to new people. This may take place in a large group, a small group or on an individual basis.

We will assume that six people are presented with the opportunity on one particular occasion, although the following would still apply if they were all seen separately.

These six people will see a business presentation *which includes a product demonstration*. What happens next is that one or two of the guests might see the potential and decide to join the network. Two or three will be happy to purchase products. The remaining one or two, if asked, may suggest certain other people who might like to see the business or the products (See Figure 1). As a result of the meeting you could:

1. Sponsor one or two people and grow your network;

2. Sell some products;

3. Get some referrals from those who did not join the business.

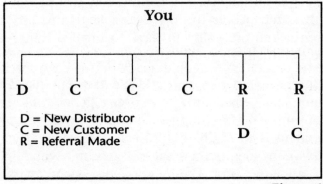

Figure 1

In this example the meeting has resulted in four customers and two new distributors. Your next steps will be to:

1. Repeat the process with another group of people;

2. Help your new distributors start the process for themselves;

3. Nurture your new customers;

4. Follow up the referrals, who may become customers or distributors.

By this time, if all goes well (and it does not always work out as neatly as the example!) you will have a team of nine, including yourself. Your first and second distributors will have begun to build a team, and there will be a total of sixteen customers.

Now you should be able to see how *everything* you need to do in order to build a productive network is contained within the activity of introducing the business opportunity to people. The sales generated in this way will be quite sufficient to enable you to qualify for any bonuses available, and for everyone involved to make some immediate profit from retailing.

All that has been said above is in no way meant to suggest that retail sales should not be pursued as a specific activity where appropriate. There will be plenty of distributors in any network who joined because they loved the products, felt happy selling them and wanted to make a limited income from doing just that. A good network opportunity should always be flexible enough to accommodate this type of person, and good networkers know the benefits of having people like this in their business.

It is also perfectly acceptable for a person who loves selling the products to concentrate on this aspect of the business and sponsor new distributors from customers who show similar enthusiasm about the products. Certainly, more sales means more profit – initially.

Our message, however, is this: substantial long-term security, profitability and growth in network marketing is more likely to be achieved by promoting the business opportunity first. Look at the charts in Figure 2. They illustrate the income growth likely to be achieved by three different people over several years of consistent part-time effort in a network business.

Anne enjoys selling and loves the products. She has no ambition to develop a large business and is happy making £500 a month from her retailing profit. Very occasionally, without conscious effort, she will meet someone just like herself who wants to do the same. The same thing will happen to the new person too. Anne's network and her earnings, will grow at a slow rate.

Betty also loves the products and enjoys selling them frequently at events she organises. She has more ambitious goals than Anne. She wants to build a big network. At every selling occasion or event she attends, she identifies prospective distributors and tries to interest them in joining her. She also asks every customer if they know anyone who would like to earn a good part-time income by doing what she is doing. Being so consistent, Betty finds one or two people every month to join her network. Gradually these new people realise the potential of building a network for themselves, and so Betty's income grows as her network steadily develops.

Cathy also has big plans. However, she has been concentrating on showing the business opportunity. Her income grows more slowly than the other two for a while, but then it begins a steep increase.

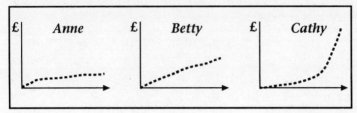

Figure 2

Let us analyse what is happening in each case. Anne's business grows very slowly because she is making no special effort to sponsor people and because the only 'message' she is sending out is: 'This is a small business for part-timers who want to make a little money from selling products to a few people'.

Betty is being far more positive and definite, inviting as many people as possible to join her team. Consequently her network, and her income, grows much faster than Anne's. However, although she makes a point of explaining the full potential of the business opportunity, actions speak louder than words. So the strongest message that she puts across is: 'You have to go out and sell quite a bit, like me.' Result – she does not reach many of those people who would be very interested in the benefits of network marketing but who do not want to go out selling as much as she does.

For the first eight or nine months Cathy's business is less profitable than the other two. She is personally selling less because she is spending more time showing the business to people. But look at the effect on her income over the longer term; during the first six months she has built the foundations for a very strong business indeed.

Something else is happening within Cathy's business which is helping to ensure her success. She is showing the business opportunity to many people who do not want to get involved in 'selling'.

The importance of revealing the full potential first

Cathy is showing the business opportunity to many more people than Anne or Betty so she is inevitably sponsoring more. But Cathy is also sponsoring people who would not have joined Anne's or Betty's team:

- People who do not think they want to get involved in selling things;
- People who like selling but want more than just retailing profits;
- Dynamic business-minded people who would not be attracted to the way Anne or Betty ran their business (i.e. with a lot of selling);
- People who would not normally be found through selling activities.

All these people are joining Cathy's business because they have been given a chance to develop different, and probably more accurate, preconceptions about what the business involves.

Those whose ambitions are too high to consider what they see as simply a selling business can see that turnover is generated as part of the process of developing a network, without selling being a separate and onerous task.

Those who do like selling should not be put off as there is a selling opportunity available too. When you build your network in this way you ensure that as many people as possible see the greatest potential in the business. The few who commit to fulfilling that potential for themselves will be the ones who will help you to get the most from your business.

The principle of duplication

Of the three, Cathy is best exploiting the principle of duplication. This is the principle used by the world's most successful businesses. The income which can be generated from one point of distribution is always finite. Every large retail chain – Marks and Spencer for example – started off with one shop. There was a limit to how much stock could pass through that outlet, and a limit to how many customers could be reached. So they opened another shop, then another, then another, and so on. Turnover and profits increased, and the potential is limited only by the number of suitably-sized towns in the country (or the world).

Franchising is a rather different method of duplication. A good franchise operation duplicates itself quickly and efficiently by offering a successful business formula to other people in return for an investment of capital and energy, and a share of the profits. The franchisor can therefore grow his business and exploit its potential faster than might otherwise have been possible.

To maximise profits, the principle is simply to get your products to as many customers as possible. Network marketing takes this principle to its ultimate conclusion. It reduces the complications of premises, equipment, stock and employees to the simplest possible method of retailing – home-based, person-to-person, small individual turnover. The profit generated by each outlet (distributor) is quite small but the potential for expansion becomes enormous. This is because of the simplicity of the duplication and the vastly greater number of people able to become involved.

Now you can visualise the possibility of a network of hundreds, thousands, even tens of thousands of individual businesses, their accumulated turnover of such size that a commission of just a small percentage adds up to a substantial income for those who did most to develop the network.

Growth and security

You might argue that if the average turnover per distributor was ten times as much you could obtain the same income from a network ten times smaller. This is true, but what of the prospects of the two networks? Figure 3 shows how the turnover of two hypothetical networks grows over a year. Both start at an overall turnover of £100,000 per month. A's network has 100 distributors averaging £1,000 per month and B's has 1,000 distributors averaging £100 per month. As a conservative estimate we will assume that each month one in fifteen of A's distributors sponsors someone new. B's distributors are spending less time on sales and more on sponsoring so we will assume a slightly greater ratio of one in ten sponsoring each month.

What has happened after a year? A's turnover has grown by 117% to £217,000 per month. But B's busi-

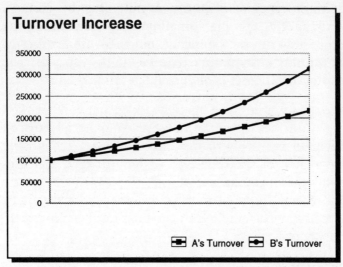

Figure 3

ness has grown twice as fast – 214% to £314,000. The greater number of people involved in B's business means that the overall turnover is more reliable and less affected by drop-outs and inactivity.

The balance between sponsoring and selling makes a crucial difference, as you have seen. This does not mean that fewer sales equals faster growth. There does come a point when sales are so low that network growth is unproductive, so the balance needs to be actively managed in any growing network. The ideal, of course, is high product sales and high sponsoring!

Investing time, not money

Working with people to build a network requires an investment of time rather than a financial investment, another reason why network marketing is so different to most types of business. Admittedly, the costs of working with people – mainly travel and telephone expenses – can be significant, but these are overheads, or running costs, rather than capital investment. The matter of expenses is discussed later in this book.

How does time investment work in network marketing? Consider first a normal salaried job (see Figure 4). Payment is weekly or monthly in arrears and further payments for the time worked are unlikely. Increases and other benefits are at the employer's discretion, and a small annual increase is often all that can be hoped for. The employee's time has not been *invested*, but *spent*.

Now consider an occupation where a product is created through unpaid work by a self-employed person;

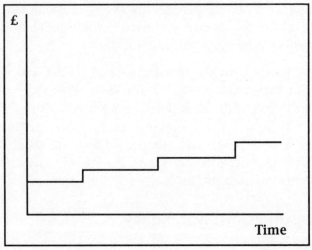

Figure 4

a writer, for example (see Figure 5). Here the payment is based not on the work done but on how many people purchase the product and for how long. This means that when the creative work has been done – when the book has been written – another one can be started while the first one is earning royalties.

Suppose one book is written each year and they all sell steadily for several years. After the first unpaid year the author can expect a steadily increasing income throughout his career. Authors *invest* their own time for a future return. They have the potential to reap a far greater return for their efforts than the employee.

Finally consider committed networkers (Figure 6). They invest their time in people. Their creation will be a network through which large quantities of products flow to end-users. Like authors, they work initially for

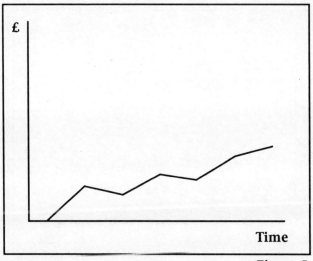

Figure 5

little immediate reward, but expect a good return on their time investment. Unlike authors, however, networkers are finding other people who also wish to invest some time in their future. The time that these people invest is simultaneously being added to the total time investment of their upline distributors.

The author's maximum time investment is 24 hours per day. Networkers have no limit because they, and others, are continually finding more people who will help them to increase the productivity of each day. It is perfectly reasonable to assume that, in due course, the networker's business can have thousands of hours input each day, every day of the year. Now that *is* exciting!

Once his business is going, the time invested by a networker gives not only a permanent return, but a return

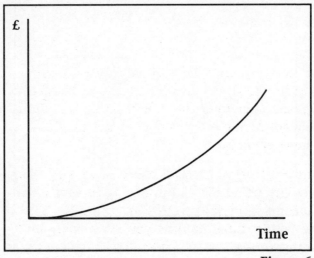

Figure 6

that continues to increase, like compound interest on a sum of money deposited in a bank. The amount of bank interest grows each year because it is paid on the original sum and the accumulated interest. Network marketing yields a continuing return on all time invested by the distributor plus a return on the time invested by other people who have joined the business.

A long term business

We hope you now have a better understanding of the fundamentals of the unique form of business called network marketing: unique because the combination of the attractive benefits and the incredibly high potential is available to such a large segment – a majority – of the population.

Individuals are complicated and unpredictable, but averages of large numbers of people are much more reliable. This is why your network must be developed to a size large enough to smooth out individual variations in performance. This is often (though not necessarily) a fairly slow process which can only be speeded up by increasing either the time invested in building the network or the effectiveness of the time already being invested, or both.

Building a successful network has to be seen as a long term activity rather than a business to provide a 'full-time' income from day one. If you are making a good income within three months you're probably doing something wrong; too much selling or recruiting at the expense of teaching others. This will become clearer later as we describe what happens when you start to build your network.

Action agenda

With the help of your sponsor:

1. Write down the names of ten people you will show your business to, in the next five days.

2. State the amount of sales you will regularly achieve, and teach your team to achieve:

   £................ (retail value)

Chapter 4

How to harness 'people power'

Making your £1,000,000 definitely requires a firm grasp of how people work in the environment of network marketing, and how to treat them for the best mutual long term success. Possibly not every high-earning networker will use the approach we suggest; however, we commend it to you as a way to build a strong, ethical and satisfying business.

All businesses are run by people who supply goods or services to other people. That is nothing new, but is not what we mean by a 'people business'.

Look again at one of the vital characteristics of network marketing; the numbers of people involved, the fact that the distributors are mostly part-time, working from home, turning over only a small amount per month. There are far more people involved per £1,000,000 of turnover than almost any other type of business. It takes a while for most people, especially those with business experience, to fully grasp how much of a people business network marketing really is. The usual perception of business is the buying and selling of things, with people being the necessary tools to do the marketing and selling. In network marketing, people are the building blocks: we are looking for people, not sales. The sales will happen almost automatically as we find our building blocks and bind them together with a strong mortar of knowledge, enthusiasm and commitment.

The most important part of a successful network marketing business is the interaction between the people involved. To build a productive network you will need 'people skills'. You need not worry if you are not confident about your skills, they can be learned from your upline and from books and tapes.

The need for people skills comes from the two fundamentals of network marketing; finding people and teaching them. You need the ability to interact positively with people at every opportunity and to teach them how to release *their* potential people skills.

In network marketing we are looking for people who are searching for a way to improve their lifestyles, their lives, their self-confidence. They have been inspired by the potential they see in network marketing. Most are not fully confident that they can succeed. They may face scepticism and pessimism from their friends and acquaintances. Possibly they would not achieve their goals if they were left to do it alone.

Most people who start a network marketing business for the first time need help to build their confidence and skills. Even if they understand *what* they need to do, they may not be sure *how* they are going to do it. They are often afraid of failing.

New networkers may have great confidence in their successful sponsor, they may have great confidence in their company, and they may love the products. But despite all they may have heard about the potential of network marketing, they will probably start their business not quite believing it. It takes time and gradual understanding for most people to become completely confident that the potential is real.

The one thing that new networkers are least confident about is their own ability. Developing self-confidence, self-discipline and belief in their own ability to succeed is often the task that can take longer than anything else.

It could be *you* we are talking about. It certainly will be true of most of the people you bring into your network, and that is why people skills are so important. Your sponsor, their sponsor, and so on (your upline) might need to help you increase your own self-confidence. They should work with you for long enough to demonstrate that *you* can do what they have learnt to do. They will probably work with your downline distributors too, until you are ready to take over. It is then up to you to pass on your training and experience to your people in exactly the same way.

If you want a conventional job you will first have to find one on offer. Then you will have to apply for it, which means you will have to show your prospective employer that you have the qualities, experience and qualifications required. This might get you an interview, during which you will have to convince them that you are the best candidate for the position. It is likely that your desire and determination to get the job will count for much less than your past performance, your track record.

If, on the other hand, you want to get into business as an independent distributor for a network marketing company you will have to demonstrate absolutely nothing to anyone except your ability to find the very modest start-up cost. Your past is irrelevant; your plans for the future are what count.

In a job you may be one of a number of people with a similar job description. There will be people with a higher status than you to control what you do, and there may be people who answer to you. In network marketing everyone has the same job to do. The normal business works when everyone does their own particular job properly. Network marketing works when everyone does exactly the same job. Duplication is everything. It is not 'Do what I say', but 'Do what I do'.

Setting an example is the most powerful teaching you can give. The simpler you can make your own activities, the easier it is for your team to say 'I can do that', and the more often they will actually do it. *Success = Simplicity*.

You must foster the 'I can do that' attitude. New distributors start by looking at what their sponsor does. If the sponsors' activities are simple and repeatable and their attitudes desirable and achievable then the new distributors are primed for success. They need only to add the commitment.

Just as important as sponsoring is teaching. Teaching is what allows duplication to happen. Sponsoring and moving products happen very effectively when friendly, mutually rewarding relationships are developed regularly with new people, be they customers or potential distributors.

There are benefits in learning specific techniques for finding and recruiting prospects, but by far the most effective tool for succeeding with people is your attitude. A positive attitude will attract people to you and make them glad they got to know you. Specific techniques will only suit a certain set of circumstances, but everyone can develop, or change, their attitudes. This is why you are likely to find that your upline, and possibly the network marketing company too, promote self-improvement materials to their network of distributors. Improving the way you deal with people generally is the most productive training you can give yourself.

Now we will look at the two groups of people with whom you will be dealing throughout the life of your business: your business associates and your customers.

Your business associates

Your success in network marketing depends on bringing new people into your network and at the same time making it work. Both of these activities rely almost completely on your ability to deal with people. Of course you also need to know about your company, your products and how the bonuses work. But if you know how *people* work you are going to have a head start. Don't worry if you think: 'I'm not very good with people'. You can learn.

Building your network

Your first task in network marketing is to start building your network. This is going to involve speaking to people you know to see if they would be interested in doing what you are doing. They will not all be interested but the more people you get to know, the more people you can speak to and the more you will find who *are* interested.

You already know a lot of people, and you know of even more. In a few years' time you will have a thriving network consisting mainly of people you did not know when you got started. The key principle here is to get to know as many people as possible. How do you do that? By becoming someone who likes people. What we mean is developing an interest, a fascination, in people: study them, ask questions, find out what makes them tick.

Making people your hobby is great fun and a source of endless enjoyment and inspiration. It is also the most effective way of building your network. Everyone has an interesting story to tell about themselves and most people love telling it to anyone who will listen. When you ask the right questions you will find that most people are not completely happy with their lot. They want to do more things than they can afford, they want more money, more time with their family, they dislike their job, they always wanted a business but never had the capital. Talk to people and – more importantly – *listen* to people, and you will find that many are virtually asking to be given an opportunity like the one you can offer.

Rosa had joined a network and was not only quite new to the area where she was living, she was quite new to the country. Many people would consider this an insurmountable problem, but Rosa liked people and knew that she would soon have many friends. But she needed to speed up the process, so she joined an evening class to study a subject she was very interested in. This was obviously a perfect place to meet people with similar interests, and that is exactly what she did. She found that several of the other students had similar financial ambitions to her and she sponsored six of them into her business within a few weeks.

Anyone can start a conversation and ask a few questions, but it is even easier to talk to people whom you know have similar interests to you.

Network marketing is a self-selection process. You do not choose who enters and succeeds in your business (although you have the choice *not* to offer the opportunity to someone you would rather not work with). People select themselves when they have been given the opportunity. Your responsibility is to give them the opportunity. Not to convince or persuade, but to explain. The progress of your business is directly proportional to the number of people to whom you offer the opportunity.

The essence of all businesses is that they will be successful if they help enough people get what they want. Everyone gets satisfaction by being able to help someone out when they can. How do you feel about being able to offer someone an opportunity which could be just what they have been looking for for years but did not ever expect to find? You can get really well paid in network marketing for helping people get what they want! You are going to have to take your mind off the subject of *you* and what you want, and get switched on to finding out what others want and showing them how to go about getting it.

Making it work

It is great to see your network begin to grow, to see the first tangible evidence of the exciting future ahead. But it will not keep growing all by itself. That is because it is composed of real people, and people do not or cannot always do what you want them to do when you want them to do it. Often they do not even do what they say they will. At heart, we know this. We all know people who are not reliable, punctual or many other things we would like them to be. None of our friends are perfect, but we pass over the characteristics we dislike and accept them for the characteristics we do like.

The difference with people who join your network is that their characteristics have a direct bearing on your business success. You will have to put up with them, though, because they are under no compulsion to run their own businesses the way you want them to. What is the answer to this frustrating problem?

First you must realise that it is not actually a problem. It is just the way things are: it is human nature, an unalterable fact of life which simply has to be dealt with.

So, how *do* we deal with it? We create an environment of support, motivation and information. You will never get people to do things simply because you want them to. What you *can* do is create the perfect conditions for nurturing any desire that people might have to do things for themselves.

If your company's network is well-established the good thing is that you do not have to do this yourself to start with because the support system should already

be in place – you should have plenty of upline distributors to help you. You will probably need their support as much as your new people if you are fairly new
to the game. Being a sole trader can be a lonely business. It is easy to get knocked back by some of the
responses you will undoubtedly get about your products and your business opportunity. You are going to
need to be around some positive and successful people
on a regular basis. It will revitalise you to know that
everyone else has to deal with the same things that get
you down, and that plenty of people have got where
you want to be by dealing with ten times the number
of setbacks you have had.

Your customers

A typical retailing business finds its customers through
advertising, retail premises, direct mail, telesales, mail
order and many other ways. In all of these methods it
is rare that a friendly personal relationship exists or is
created through the process of making the sale. It is
usually impossible or impractical for the seller to
develop a close relationship with the customer due to
distance or sheer numbers of customers. In any case it
is unlikely that the seller – the person who physically
deals with the sale – has any reason to be motivated to
make that extra effort.

Now look at network marketing businesses. There are
two big differences in the way that retail customers are
supplied through network marketing compared to
most other marketing methods.

1. There are many more sellers. In network marketing
   the ratio of sellers to customers is generally some-

where between 1:10 and 1:100. A conventional retailing business could have a ratio anywhere between, say, 1:500 (e.g. a village greengrocer) and 1:10,000 (e.g. a mail order company).

2. The customers are usually personally known by the sellers. If not, they are likely to be friends of an existing customer.

With a typical company you can build a profitable and secure network business if you and every one of your distributors finds and services just 20 customers a month. They might be the same people every month if you have consumable products. On the other hand you might need only one or two customers a month if you are dealing with higher value items. It makes good sense, then, to really look after your customers. If you do this and keep in touch with them, they can be a constant source of referrals and they may buy any future products offered by your company. As a customer, do you not prefer to be one of 20 rather than one of 50,000? Do you like to feel very highly valued for your custom? Do you like 'no quibble' guarantees and free samples? Would you appreciate prompt, free and friendly home delivery at any time on any day of the week that suits you?

If I need a carpet fitting I will employ a friend of mine whom I know will do a quality job at a good price. If I want any financial advice I will go first to a trusted friend in that business. Everyone likes to do business with people they trust, especially if they are also friends. Your network business is therefore about making friends.

Forget that ridiculous phrase: 'I couldn't sell to my friends', which you will hear often enough. If 'sell to' means 'rip off', 'pester' or 'bore' then no one in their right mind would do it to their friends. But you are going to treat these people like VIPs and they are going to love it!

My wife gives her customers a 'collector card' which contains twelve squares. As a 'thank you' to them she will sign a square every time they spend £10 with her, and when the squares are filled she gives them £20 worth of products free. Her customers *always* come to her first. See what we mean about this being a 'people' business?

People have problems

A people business is not all plain sailing. The fact that you and your team will inevitably develop a close relationship also means that you are likely to become involved to some extent in their personal lives. Everyone faces challenges throughout their lives. Life itself is a challenge. In the first paragraph of his book *The Road Less Travelled*, M. Scott Peck states:

> *'Life is difficult. Once we truly know that life is difficult – once we truly understand and accept it – then life is no longer difficult. Because once it is accepted, the fact that life is difficult no longer matters.'*

If you can fully appreciate this you will have taken a giant leap which will benefit you and your team.

Going into a new and totally different environment, however risk-free it may be, is a big challenge for most people. Their previous working experience will not normally prepare them for what lies ahead, for example the number of rejections they will get. These will only be rejections of the products or the business, not of the person, but they can be tough to take at first – and even when you are used to it!

This and other challenges must be overcome for new distributors to become successful; they must become positively motivated. This is where your company and upline's support system comes into play. The 'system' is the backbone of your business and consists of the functions, the trainings, the recognitions, the newsletters, the videos, the audio tapes, the recommended books – a constant drip-feeding of positive motivation and inspiration.

Some people do not need the system and can get going effectively by themselves. Others could not survive or even get started in the business without it. Many people have signed up as distributors for a network company and done nothing for a year *except* plug into the system. After this period everything fell into place for them and they went on to become highly successful in the business. Take the example of Sharon and Andrew.

I met Andrew when I answered an advertisement for a filing cabinet that I saw in our local Co-op store. Like me, he worked from home. He was very friendly and helped me to get the cabinet home. A few days later, when we had planned our first business opportunity meeting at home, I decided to call Andrew and invite him. Being open-minded and always ready to look at an opportunity, he was happy to come. Of the six people present at the meeting, only Andrew was interested in the business. He went home, discussed it with his wife Sharon, and they decided to join. Their first home meeting was not too successful, and they both had the challenge of working such long hours full-time that they saw very little of each other. Nothing much happened for the next eight months except that they went to as many functions as they could, read relevant books and our newsletters, listened to tapes and attended the conference. Significantly, they watched us develop our business and begin to get somewhere. Then one day Sharon telephoned. She had decided to quit her highly stressful job and build her network business full-time. Andrew is still in a very demanding job, but 100% behind Sharon, who is totally committed to making her business work and has a team of around 100 people which is daily growing stronger.

What about the daily task of developing your network, your people? They will have difficulties and they will tell you about them, especially when they prevent them from performing in their business as well as they had planned. You cannot solve all their problems but you can provide a support system for their network business. If they have made some progress and then find they have to stop work for a period you can help keep their business going. After all, it is your business too. In any case, you can let them go and sort out their problems knowing that when they come back they will be welcomed and offered the same support as before.

Knowing that you are there behind them, supporting them in all their efforts is what locks people into your business. To some people the social aspect is more attractive than the business potential. You will notice them coming to every meeting but never quite getting started. But you never know, sometimes they do.

In a people business you have to be prepared for anything. People do the strangest things. You will be puzzled, frustrated, let down and exasperated by a large proportion of your team and by an even larger proportion of your prospects. Every now and then, however, you will find a bright star who will inspire and motivate you, who will help to make all your efforts worthwhile. Then you really will know why we call this a people business.

In the following chapters we will examine in more detail how the peculiarities of people make an impact upon your business as it develops.

Action agenda

1. List three ways in which you can really look after your customers:

   i)...
   ....

   ii)..
   ....

   iii)...
   ....

How do you think they will repay
you?..
....

2. List three ways in which you can really look after
   the people in your network:

   i)...
   ....

   ii)..
   ....

   iii)...
   ....

3. In the long run, what will be the effect of doing
   these things?...
   ....

Chapter 5

Success is a numbers game

This is perhaps the one area where network marketing is very similar to other businesses. Every business has the task of finding, from the vast numbers of the general population, that proportion who want the products or services they have for sale. If your goal is to make £1,000,000 through network marketing you will have to find just a few of that proportion of the population who want what your business can offer them; just a few people with similar goals to you. They are there, but you have to play the numbers game in order to find them!

People ask, with good reason: 'Why do so many fail in network marketing?' A wary potential distributor may follow up with a related question: 'If only a small percentage make good money what chance is there for me?' We are going to answer these questions fully here, but please bear in mind that similar questions can be asked about any other form of business or any other project that requires effort and persistence. Also you should consider what 'fail' means in the context of network marketing. It certainly does not mean incurring thousands of pounds worth of debt or going bankrupt. All it means is wasting some time and incurring a certain amount of normal business expenses (mainly travel and telephone).

You have probably heard of the 80:20 rule, which fairly accurately describes human nature in all manner of situations. It says that in any endeavour 20% of the people achieve 80% of the results. It follows that on average the 20% work sixteen times more productively than the 80%. That is the reality when you deal with people, and – because this is a people business – that is the reality with network marketing.

Having said that, we feel that there are still too many people not achieving their goals in this business. They are failing because they have been poorly prepared for the realities of what happens when they start to build a network. Too many business opportunity presentations have misled people into thinking everything happens much faster and much more easily than is actually the case.

When keen new distributors get their tenth rejection before sponsoring anyone they may begin to think it is not going to work. By that time it might be too late to tell them the whole story. What follows below, and elsewhere in this book, is information that we think you should know before you get going, because we want you to be prepared and to be a winner.

Contacting

We are going to back up what we say here with some real statistics from a live and growing network business. This is obviously only a single example, but I believe the figures are typical and give a good indication of what to expect. We will start right at the begin-

	Contact	Apt	Joined
Graham Bisham			
Jenny (dentist)	488672	✓	✗
Mrs Kettle	011313	✓	✗
~~Kurt Jaguara~~	~~0882451716~~		
K Steve Bulone	0151 255 2020	✓ ✓	✗
Ken Green	555705	✓ ✓	✗
Joan + Angie (letter)	434204	✓	✗
Charles Pross	870543		
Graham Costa - letter		✓	✓ ✓
~~Ben Emsden~~ - "			
S Eriksen		✓	✗
A Gerard		✓	✗
~~McClellan~~ - ~~letter~~		✓ ✓	✗
Nixon (reception)			
A Nicoll			
Mike + Tracy		✓	✗
Mary S		✓	✗
Rick Moore		✓	✗
Brian Evans	033 920 6170	✗	
~~Delia Gaymer~~	~~053571717~~		
~~Brian Newcomb~~	~~0765 216321~~		
R Hinson			
Mike Kenny (Better worse)	230456	✓	✗
Barber		✓	✗
C + R Wright		✓	✗
Judy Thompson	396213	✓ ✓	✗
Researcher (J Wood)		✓	✗
Brian Queen	01547 267443	✓ ✓	✓
Debbie Tanner		✓ ✓	✗
B Taylor	01863 673820	✓ ✓	✓
Greengrocer (Terry)		✓	✗
~~Steve Spiegel~~	~~081 482 7008~~	✗	
A Wordsmith (ACG)	0494 651944	✓ ✓	✗
Gill Street - when less busy	648313	✓ ✓	
P. Hewett (MD of Nixon's)	252568	✓ ✓	✗
Brian Loss (MD, NRT)	117895	✓ ✓	✗
Gavin Turnpike	840213	✓ ✓	✗

Figure 7

ning with the prospect (or contact) list. This is a list of everyone you know and everyone you know of. It is the first thing your sponsor will tell you to do when you join a network; the job that 80% of distributors do not do (remember the 80:20 rule?). The prospect list in my example has 230 names on it and three columns to the right of each name. In the first column is a tick by each person who has been contacted. There are 195 ticks.

In the second column is a further tick if the person contacted has agreed to look at the business by coming to a meeting, making an appointment or simply watching a video or reading a book. In the second column there are 85 ticks, so 44% of those contacted were interested enough to take a look.

In the third column is a final tick if the person has looked at the business, liked it, and decided to get involved. There are nineteen ticks in the third column, so in this case about 22% of those looking at the business actually joined. To put it another way, 10% of the people contacted signed up as distributors.

Now look at how these nineteen people performed once they got into the business. Three never did a thing and eventually dropped out. Six had a flurry of activity for a short time and then gave up, for whatever reason. Three were still saying they intended to get going a year after they started. Five turned out to be consistent low-level retailers who occasionally sponsored someone. Two made real commitments and are on their way to becoming leaders within their company's network. So approximately 10% of those joining really go for it.

Only 1% of those contacted turned out to be high achievers. If we class the other 99% as failures (which is not true because some of them are performing exactly to the level they had planned) then our first question – 'Why do so many fail?' – is answered; they choose to. Every one of the people contacted had the same opportunity offered to them. Only two chose to take full advantage of it. The second question – 'What chance is there for me?' – is also answered; every possible chance. Network marketing, and every other opportunity, rewards those who choose to take on the challenge.

Look at this 1% again. Although it seems to be simply too low to be viable, it certainly is not! Look at the marketing plan (commission structure) for your company's network; how many high achievers do you need to qualify for the bonuses that will give you a substantial income? It will probably be between four and six – say five. Going by the figures we have seen above you will need to contact about 500 people. That sounds daunting, but how long will it take you? At only one telephone call a day it will take you less than two years to find them yourself. Most proprietors of start-up businesses would give their eye teeth to have a business with a six-figure profit potential after only two years without having taken any financial risk in the meantime. If you are wondering where you are going to find 500 people to contact, we will cover this in a later chapter, but at this stage we can assure you it is perfectly practical.

What often happens, though, is that other people find some of your high achievers for you. A good sales and marketing plan allows your five high achievers to be anywhere 'downline' in your network, *as long as they are in separate legs of your business*. Any successful networkers will tell you that they did not personally find all of their best people.

Now look at the other 99% again. All is not lost with these people. Of the 176 who did not look at or join the business first time around, some will have different circumstances at some stage in the future and might want to take another look. Similarly, one or two of the inactive distributors will probably become active after a period. One or two of the people introduced by the low achievers might show great potential. Your 1% could just possibly become 1.5% or even double to 2%, and that would make a tremendous difference to your income in the long term!

What have you learnt? We hope you are beginning to understand that the development of your network is completely dependent on the numbers game even though your success is assured the moment you make a commitment. We hope you will not be disappointed, irritated, angry and demotivated by the responses you will certainly get from many people as you go about the necessary process of contacting them. The result of any particular action you take is insignificant, however high your hopes are for the outcome. The only thing that matters is that you continue the process. Eventually the numbers will work in your favour.

Network building

The statistics of what happens within your network as you build it are not only quite fascinating but extremely useful to know in advance. In this section we hope to counter the unrealistic attitudes which some people, perhaps you, have as a result of being shown a very simplified illustration of how the business works. How many times have you heard: 'You find five people, then they find five each...' and so on. It sounds easy, but that is not quite how it works. Being realistic does not mean being pessimistic; on the contrary, it means knowing what to expect and accepting it when it happens. Then you can get on with doing the right things for success in the long term.

Again, we'll pick on our real live business and see how the figures stack up. The chart overleaf (Figure 8) shows the number of people personally sponsored each month over a three year period. It does not show the numbers of people who become inactive, resign or fail to renew their distributorship.

What can we learn from this? The average number of people sponsored per month is two and a half. Many will be able to work much faster than this, others will be slower, there is no right number. No new people were sponsored between the 21st and 23rd months, after a productive period of sponsoring between the 10th and the 19th months, when 33 were sponsored. A break from sponsoring was taken in favour of a period of consolidation, spent helping and training these new people to start developing their businesses effectively. There is no point in sponsoring so many people that you cannot spend the time needed to help them get started properly.

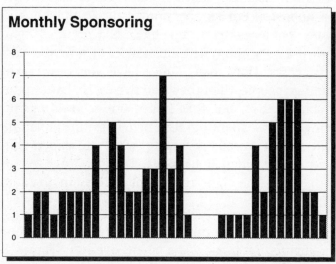

Monthly Sponsoring

Figure 8

The next figure (Figure 9) shows the total number of people in the network, month by month over the same three year period. This chart does take account of 'drop-outs'.

People sometimes talk about the 'geometric' growth possible in network marketing. In case this term is unfamiliar to you, it means that the speed of growth keeps increasing in an upward curve, whereas in 'arithmetical' growth the speed of growth stays the same, in a straight line. So if you sponsored two people every month but no one else did, your team would grow arithmetically. If you and everyone else in your team sponsored two a month the size of your team would increase geometrically. In fact, it would triple in size every month and in eighteen months there would be 387,000,000 people involved. Clearly, the true rate of growth is far lower than this, although there is evi-

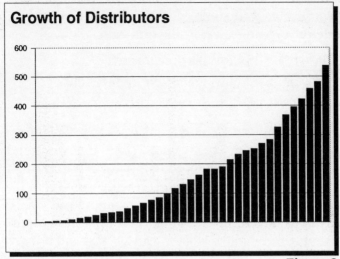

Growth of Distributors

Figure 9

dence of increasing speed of growth – the upward curve – as you can see in Figure 9.

In the particular business we are examining, the activity rate – the percentage of distributors who place an order in a given month – varies between 25% and 52%, with an overall average of 36% over the year. That may disappoint you. How much more exciting 100% activity would be! But we promised to give you the facts. What is exciting is that the average turnover per distributor per month is £90 at distributor prices (or £123 at retail value). When you are pulling out your hair because you have sponsored your first four people and none of them are doing anything it is reassuring to know that, in the long run, everyone in your network is worth £90 of turnover (or whatever the relevant figure is for your company) every month.

Another set of figures culled from this real live example will give you some idea of what overall level of activity you can expect from your team.

- 36% of distributors become inactive
- 34% of distributors are intermittently active
- 20% of distributors have consistent low activity
- 10% of distributors have consistent high activity

The final figure of 10% is virtually an 'industry standard' which seems to apply to all networks. You might ask why we are bombarding you with what seem like fairly depressing statistics; are we trying to put you off network marketing? Not at all. You now have a great advantage, you know what to expect. You will not give up when you find out that most distributors in your network do very little. You know that it is not a problem, just a fact to be aware of. You will be on your way to your £1,000,000!

In the next chapter we will look at the true costs of developing a profitable network.

Action agenda

1. Keep an accurate record of the results of your contacting. Can you improve on our example?

2. Start a conversation with someone new – today. Make a habit of it.

3. Refer back to your financial goals written at the end of Chapter 2. How many new distributors do you need to sponsor each month to achieve your goals? Discuss this with your upline.

Chapter 6

Control your costs and maximise your profits

This book is all about preparing you for a highly successful network marketing business – one which is going to earn you £1,000,000. As far as we are aware there is no other book on the subject which tells you how much you are going to have to spend before (and after) you start to receive the large bonuses you are looking forward to. There are expenses and overheads for any business, whether or not it is operated from a home. We have seen many people quit their network marketing business after three or six or twelve months because they have calculated their net profit over the period and found it to be quite low. They figure that they have so far been earning at an hourly rate less than a cleaning job would pay. Nobody told them that this might happen, so they are not prepared for it. They justify their decision to quit on the basis of these past results without looking forward to the potential of the next twelve months. For most people, network marketing is not a sprint, but a marathon.

We want you to achieve your goals. We would rather see you decide against starting a network marketing business right now than have you join up without being in possession of some of the basic financial facts of the business.

Network marketing is always hailed as the business with unlimited potential which does not need much financial investment to get started. This is quite true, and we have discussed the time investment that is needed instead. However, it is true to say that virtually everything you do in the process of building a network incurs expense. You have to know about these expenses so that you can plan for them. You will need to reinvest some of your network income in items which will make a big long-term difference to your business. We are not talking about anything like the amount of money that would normally be involved in setting up a traditional type of business with the same earning potential.

How many years will it take an average traditional business to break even? Three? Five? The networker will take a little time to break even, but it will be measured in months rather than years.

Four categories of distributor

The expenses which networkers incur will vary tremendously according to how they develop their businesses, and this will in turn depend on their circumstances at the time of joining the business. People tend to be in one of these four main categories when they decide to enter network marketing, with the most favourable first.

1. *Already financially independent.* A person who can spend as much time as they like building the business while being able to live comfortably on

their own resources for at least twelve months is in the ideal position to build a substantial network in as short a time as possible. There are not too many people in this position!

2. *Reliable income from a business or job with reasonable or flexible hours of work.* Most people who come into network marketing are in such a position, which is very favourable. A regular income removes the financial stress which can adversely affect performance. Usually evenings, weekends and holidays are available for network development.

3. *Reliable income from a business or job with long and inflexible hours of work.* It is tough to build a network in these circumstances. Few people in this situation have the vision to increase their workload even more in the medium term for the sake of financial freedom in the long term. However it is perfectly possible and has been done many times.

4. *Plenty of time, no regular income and little or no available capital.* It is possible to build a network and make enough income to live on from day one, but it would require a consistently high level of retail selling until the network bonuses begin to build up from the time spent sponsoring. There would also be the added complication of explaining to prospects that they should not follow your example unless they are in similar circumstances. A better alternative may be to get a job first and move to category two or three.

Types of expense

What kind of expenses are we talking about? Primarily travelling, telephone calls, meetings, promotional materials, postage and samples. Some people choose to advertise, an activity which can dramatically increase costs. We will consider this subject separately at the end of this chapter. We will look now at each of the main unavoidable expenses mentioned above.

Travelling. Perhaps it is possible to build a large network business without the use of a car, but it would be difficult. The flexibility of travel by road would seem to be essential in order to make the number of personal contacts necessary to develop a network effectively. The cost of fuel, maintenance, insurance and depreciation of your vehicle is likely to be the largest area of expense.

Telephone. A telephone is possibly even more essential than a car. Network marketing revolves around the telephone. It is the most efficient way of contacting people. Indeed, one could say that the success of a network business is directly proportional to the number of calls made during the life of the business. Telephone costs should be in the top three areas of expenditure.

Meetings. Meetings come in all shapes and sizes: formal and informal business presentations, network training, retail training, motivational seminars and rallies, and leadership training. At first you will need only to go to the meetings which are put on for your benefit, simply incurring travelling costs and the charge, if any, for attending. Later, as your business develops, you will want to organise and pay for your own meetings.

Sales and business aids. These are absolutely necessary to inform and motivate you and to promote your business and products. You will be sending or lending information packs, books, audio and video cassettes to interested prospects and using all kinds of leaflets and brochures every day to encourage interest in your products and business. Good network marketing companies will provide excellent quality materials at reasonable, sometimes subsidised, prices. If you want to be as effective as possible you will also make a point of investing in books and other materials to increase your knowledge of network marketing and improve your skills.

High incomes are achievable only by consistent work over a long period. Only the rare person can charge on, day after day, through rejections, disappointments and irritations, without ever getting disheartened and demotivated. This is where the books, audios and videos can help. They may be specific to your distributor organisation or company, or relating to network marketing generally, or concerned with your own personal development. Many on the market are excellent and most successful networkers would agree that fifteen minutes or more of reading and listening each day will go a long way to help keep your personal motivation high. Ask your upline for recommended titles. Company-specific audio tapes are often recordings of seminars and can range from tedious to hilarious, but all will contain many gems of advice. Not everyone needs the same amount and type of motivation, so it is wise to assess for yourself the amount you need to spend on these items.

Postage. An unavoidable but relatively minor expense.

Samples. To be as effective as possible in selling your products you will need samples in addition to product brochures and other sales aids. It goes without saying that you will use your products yourself, which is one of the most powerful methods of advertising. Depending on the type of products you are dealing with, you might want or need to have samples for displaying or for potential customers to examine or try out. New distributors should ask their sponsors what assistance they can give in this respect. A sponsor who has acquired a good range of samples over a period may well be happy to loan some of them to new distributors for an initial period to help reduce the newcomers' expenses. It is difficult to say what expenses in this category will be, due to the variety product ranges. It is complicated further by the fact that many samples will be sold off at a discount after a time.

Close to home or nationwide?

How do the costs of building a network vary with the different ways of doing it? The purpose of this chapter is to prepare you for the financial facts of starting and developing your network. Depending on your financial situation and how quickly you want to break even and start making a profit, you can decide to develop your business in one of the two ways described below, or somewhere between.

Starting locally. For most people in the early stages of their business we would recommend building a network within about an hour's travelling distance from home. Costs, especially travel and telephone, are thereby kept to a minimum. Good business and personal relationships with your team can be built due to the frequency of personal contact. Your time can be much more productive when working locally because you are not spending so much of it in your car. This is especially important for those working part-time on their business. As the team builds and establishes itself the business becomes more profitable and is able to fund some of the additional costs of longer-distance sponsoring.

A disadvantage of this approach is that good prospective distributors living at a distance are not contacted as soon as one would like, so opportunities may be missed. In such cases a safeguard is to contact them anyway to 'stake your claim'. If they do show interest you can keep in contact by telephone and mail and follow up personally when you can. You may be able to refer them to a suitably supportive group in their area if you ask your upline.

Going national. Those who are not concerned with immediate profitability and simply want to develop the largest possible business in the long term will go for maximum exposure from the start. Overheads will therefore be much higher because it is essential to maintain personal contact with new distributors if they are to have the best chance of building a strong business. It is not unheard of for a new distributor to be sufficiently self-motivated, organised and knowledgeable to be able to develop a successful business without upline assistance, but it is rare. This is a people business and the relationship between a distributor and his sponsor is one of the largest building blocks of his success. You might well enrol the support of your upline in helping to develop your long-distance groups. They will be glad to assist whenever they can, but the overall responsibility is yours.

Hard facts

What level of expenditure can you expect? It is impossible to be precise here because the amounts depend entirely on the individual distributor's actual activities.

To give you an illustration of what is likely we will again use the example of our active, growing distributorship. This business started slowly and very part-time and progressed steadily, becoming almost full-time after two years. A long-term view was taken to build throughout the UK, and the business now has strong active groups in the South, London, the Midlands, East Anglia, Yorkshire and the North West. The charts below allow us to analyse two main areas of expenditure.

Telephone. This shows business telephone use only. You can see how expenses mounted over the first three quarters of the business as the essential calls were made. Initially most of the calls were to make appointments to show the opportunity or the products. As this type of call settled down from a peak in the first three months it was supplemented by a growing number of calls to existing and new distributors in order to keep in touch, arrange meetings and offer advice. The

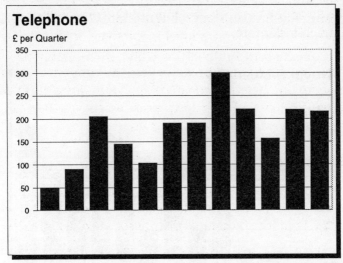

Figure 10

fourth and fifth quarters showed a further reduction in calls to prospects as more time was spent helping keen distributors to build their networks. An increase in the sixth quarter showed the need to keep in touch with more developing leaders. The eighth quarter was something of an anomaly due to a period of product distribution problems. Future costs are likely to stabilise at around £200 per quarter.

Travelling. These expenses cover all business vehicle costs, bus, train and taxi fares, and all other costs related to holding and attending meetings, accommodation and meals away from home. The pattern of growth is obvious from the chart, and is to be expected as the time input was fairly minor at the beginning, rising to virtually full-time after two years. In this time the network has developed around the country. The figures are likely to continue to rise slowly as the network develops, but income will rise at a much faster rate.

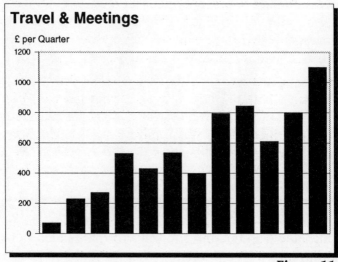

Figure 11

Sales and business aids. There is no chart for these costs, because spending on these items is too variable and individual to be able to give a typical example. However, it is useful to know what items this category would cover, some of which you might not have considered. Remember that everything was not purchased in the first week, but accumulated over a two year period.

The items included: training manuals, product leaflets, brochures, catalogues, display materials, business starter kits, promotional books, audios, videos, information packs, products for demonstration, display or loan, customer and distributor incentives, business stationery, presentation equipment and motivational books, audios and videos.

It is virtually impossible to relate expenditure on these items directly to any specific level of sales or sponsoring success. All one can confidently say is that the more people who are exposed to your business opportunity, the more successful it will be.

Here is a true story of the usefulness of promotional literature. Loretta was a networker who received a letter, on an unrelated subject, from a business acquaintance. With the letter was a promotional leaflet and a note: 'Thought you'd be interested to know that we're involved with this excellent network company'. Six weeks after receiving it, Loretta called the acquaintance to say: 'Your network marketing business looks interesting, can you send me some more details?' She soon joined the business and immediately sponsored a friend who became one of the company's most successful distributors.

The point is that you can never tell how you are going to find your superstars. The only certainty is that you will find them if you show the opportunity to enough people. The telephone is your most valuable tool for this job, but promotional materials come a close second.

Profit and loss

We have looked in some detail at specific areas of expense involved in the development of a network. Now we can take a look at what happens when all the expenses are considered together, along with all the income from personal sales and bonuses on sales of

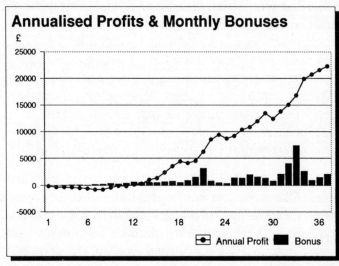

Figure 12

the network. The graph above (Figure 12) relates to the same business we have been examining and shows the profit (before tax) over the previous twelve months. For comparison purposes it also shows bonuses received each month. So if you look at month 12 you will see the business's first full year's profit. Month 30 shows a profit of £12,426 since month 18, and so on. Charting the figures in this way allows you to compare incomes with, say, a salary or other type of annual income.

Remember we are looking at profits here. Often you will hear of gigantic bonus cheques being received by top networkers. Some of them certainly are big, but they are rarely all profit. What are they spending on travelling, meetings, advertising, etc. to make possible a cheque of that size? When you look at this graph you are seeing what is left after all expenses of running the business are accounted for, and that makes the figures much more meaningful. Items included in the figures and not already mentioned are: purchase and sale of products; some advertising; purchase and sale of business kits, conference tickets; registration and renewal fees; costs of attending charity events, exhibitions, etc.; incentives and rewards for downline; business stationery; accountancy; heating, lighting, cleaning, etc.

Note that the maximum loss at any point was only £800. Okay, we are not saying that the first year's profit – £136 – will make anyone rich, but remember this was a very part-time occupation for the first twelve months. The significance of this graph is how clearly it shows the principle of investing time and only a little money at the start and reaping the benefits later. In this case it took perhaps too long to break even, but what happens afterwards is exciting. After the first year the annual profit increased at a steady average of around £800 per month. That is equivalent to a pay rise of £10,000 a year, every year!

The essence of network marketing

This is what network marketing is all about: not investing large sums of money but putting in the hours, consistently, over a period of time until the statistics begin to work. Those first six to twelve months play havoc with people who expect quick results.

Our advice is to put the blinkers on, ignore all results and do what you're supposed to do for a year. When you look up you'll have a business.

How do you know when those break even and rapid growth points are approaching? It will be different for different people, different products and different companies. In our example the break even point came when the number of distributors in the network was 57. In our experience, reliable income and steady growth comes when a network reaches about 200 distributors. The figures you have seen above illustrate very clearly why network marketing is not ideally suited to someone who needs to live on the income from the start. Estimates differ as to how long it takes to make an income you can live on, but we would suggest that, realistically, for most people twelve months is the minimum period. After all, it can take that long for people to gain enough confidence in the business and in themselves to be able to develop it effectively. We have all heard stories of almost instant wealth through network marketing, but to build a very profitable network in a short time requires concentrated effort and great determination. It needs all the work that another person might complete in a year to be concentrated into a few months. If you are willing and able to do this – to work single-mindedly and effectively for sixteen hours a day, seven days a week – you too can earn substantial bonus cheques within a few months.

Now you know what to expect. You will not fret if you are not making big money after working part-time for three, six, nine or twelve months. You know it will come if you keep doing what is necessary. Now you can prepare yourself for substantial profits in year two, three, four and beyond. Or perhaps you can do much better in your business than the one you have just examined!

Advertising

Advertising may appear to be a very tempting option to get your business opportunity in front of a large number of people in a short period of time. It is so tempting, in fact, that many people pour a lot of money into it at a very early stage without fully appreciating the consequences. Advertising can be a useful addition to your sponsoring activities but it must be treated with a great deal of caution if one is not to waste considerable sums of money. Here, we will examine some pros and cons of advertising for distributors.

Advantages. Advertising – in the right way, in the right places, at the right time – can quickly attract many people to look at your business. It expands your range of contacts to include those people whom you might never have met through other activities. Advertising can therefore speed the growth of your network by reducing the time it could take you to find the high-performance individuals you are looking for.

Disadvantages. The cost of large-scale national advertising can be extremely high. Local advertising is not cheap either. You might pay up to £10 a day for a four line classified advertisement in your local daily newspaper. A small display advertisement in a national daily for one day could cost 50 or 100 times as much. The cost of the advertisement itself, however, is only half the story.

Responses from interested readers of your advertisement need to be dealt with very quickly and professionally, for maximum results. This means that there must be someone virtually waiting by the telephone for the whole time that the advertisement is active. Rarely will respondents be ready to join you after merely replying; they will invariably ask for an information pack. For each person you will need to make up an impressive pack of literature (and, ideally, a personal letter) which puts across the business opportunity in a favourable light. The time this takes is substantial, and the cost of literature, stationery and postage will not be less than £1 per respondent. If you include items such as video cassettes the costs escalate considerably, especially as the majority will not be returned. After a suitable interval, a follow-up call is necessary (they rarely call you back!), and this adds further expense. A face-to-face meeting should be arranged with those who indicate serious interest in joining and the cost of this will vary. If you have advertised nationally, the responses could have come from anywhere in the country.

You might be quite happy to bear all these costs as an investment in the possibility of finding one or two of your future superstars. After all, even one serious business builder will eventually give you an excellent return on your outlay, even though the day when your business breaks even and starts to make good profits will be put back quite considerably.

The biggest drawback with advertising is that it is not simple, cheap, duplicatable and reliable. If you build your business by advertising, your downline distributors will want to follow your example. You may have the means to invest in costly advertising. They may not have the means, but may still believe that they should follow your example. A business which should be inexpensive to start and quick to break even begins to turn into a business which requires much more financial investment and takes much longer before going into profit.

If you feel that advertising for distributors must be a part of your sponsoring activities, we offer the following advice:

1. Only do it with money you can afford to lose if the response is poor.

2. Start locally to save advertising and travelling costs.

3. Advertising is a specialised skill. Before you commit to any significant outlays, learn all you can through reading, and ask experienced uplines for advice.

4. Always consider how you might obtain favourable editorial coverage for your business instead of or in addition to, advertising. Positive editorial is far more effective than advertising because it allows you to expand on your story, and, of course, it is also free! It is also perceived as less biased than advertising.

5. Make sure that the text of your advertisement is relevant to the readership. Talk to them in their own terms.

6. Be aware of the circulation figures of the publication; are they independently verified? Or are you taking a risk with a brand new magazine? Is it a

subscription-only publication or does it grace the shelves of newsagents around the country? Ask yourself: 'What proportion of the readers are going to be interested in my opportunity?'

7. The fewer words there are in your advertisement, the more responses you will get and the lower the quality of respondents. Sifting through them for those with potential could consume vast amounts of your time and energy. Instead, we would suggest being fairly wordy in order to pinpoint the type of respondent you want. This saves time and effort but reduces the number of enquiries.

8. Finally, don't get hooked on advertising. It's far less easy and more expensive to duplicate than talking to people.

Action agenda

1. If you have not done so already, start keeping income and expenditure records.

2. Aim to sponsor ten distributors locally before venturing further afield.

3. Sponsor at least ten people, and show your team how to do the same, before you consider advertising.

Chapter 7

Get your attitude right!

What is attitude? It is your disposition to what happens to you; your reaction to your circumstances; how you think. In particular, it is what determines how other people perceive and react to you. Without exaggeration, your attitude is crucial to your success and happiness in every aspect of your life. Your attitude has a significant effect on everything you do and everyone you meet. In a people business, therefore, it has a major impact on your progress. It can speed you or impede you as you work towards your financial goals and could literally make a difference of years in the time it takes you to achieve £1,000,000 through your network marketing business.

The good news is that if the attitude you have is not as good as it could be, you *can* change it. Some examples will illustrate the importance and effect of attitudes.

Bill had a negative attitude. He started a network marketing business with a new company. He had a little experience in the field and he felt that his new company's sales and marketing plan was not quite right – totally wrong, in fact. It seemed to him that he would have to work quite hard to qualify for the various bonuses, and then continue to work quite hard even when he reached the higher positions. Bill brought the matter up at every opportunity. It did not seem to occur to him that no one else had a problem with the plan – he assumed they had not studied it properly.

There were audible groans every time Bill spoke up at a meeting. His sponsor began to avoid him whenever possible. Bill stopped sponsoring; he did not feel able to introduce people until the plan was right. His sales started to go down because his customers did not seem to want the products quite so much after a while. This confirmed Bill's earlier suspicions that the products were too expensive.

It began to look as if the company would never sort itself out properly (i.e., to Bill's satisfaction) so Bill decided to resign. No one heard much of Bill after that, but many people heard about the company he left. It grew steadily more successful, as did all it's distributors who worked hard. Today the marketing plan is still virtually the same as it was in Bill's days with the company.

Sue had a problem with sponsoring. She said she was no good at it and that no one took her seriously. She was fine when it came to close friends and family who knew her and gave her every encouragement, but when it came to speaking to men she was stuck. They just would not take her seriously, she felt. If only her husband would join the business, she said, things would be so much easier.

Sharon made a decision, eight months after she signed up for a network marketing opportunity, that she was going to get on with it. Every possible setback that could happen, happened. Every obstacle made her more determined to make the business work. Two years later she began to receive worthwhile bonuses, and in all that time her sponsors never once heard her say: 'I quit', 'I can't do it' or 'I don't think this is going to work'. Sharon's sponsors, downline and customers always look forward to seeing her because her smile, enthusiasm and determination are infectious.

Robert had a highly successful sales business which went spectacularly bust. He had always liked the idea of building a network marketing business and this was the opportunity he had been waiting for. He knew he would not be picking up substantial cheques for a year or so and he had some plans to keep a roof over his head and food on the table, but it was not easy. Robert's circumstances are just about the most difficult you could imagine for someone building a network, but you would never guess so if you met him. His sincerity, warmth, genuine enthusiasm and love of people inspire everyone he meets. At any meeting people gravitate to him because he makes them feel good about the business and themselves.

There you have four very different profiles. Which of them would you like to have in *your* business? Who will build tremendous networks? Which of the four get to meet the most people and hence the most potential distributors and customers? The only real difference between the first two individuals and the last two is their attitudes – what they think and how they react to what happens around them. If you want to make good progress in network marketing you need to have the right attitude...

...a positive and professional attitude

Here's how a positive and professional attitude will benefit you in your network building. Remember, this is not hype or conjecture but is based on real experiences of people in network marketing. We already know that network marketing is a people business. This frightens some because they think that they do not know enough people. They are right, they do not know enough people. But the point is not how many people you know, rather it is:

1. The people you know of;

2. The people they know and know of; and most significantly:

3. The people you will get to know and the people they will get to know.

It will be your positive and professional attitude which will allow you to get to know so many people throughout the life of your business. You will create a lasting impression on everyone you meet. They will take away a good feeling about you which if put into words would be something like: 'Hey, I could get on with her', or 'Yes, I could do business with someone like that', or simply: 'I like him'.

Sooner or later you might approach that person about your business. It could be the next day. It could be five years later. It could be someone you knew at college 20 years ago. When you make that call you'll say: 'Hi John, it's Joe Smith here' and John is going to take a second or two to remember who Joe Smith is. When he does he is going to be pleased you called and receptive to what you have to say. And that increases your chance of a successful approach.

John agrees to come to a business presentation. Perhaps he would not have done so but for the fact that he thought: 'If Joe's involved it must be worth looking at. In any case I'd like to see Joe again.' John comes and listens to an enjoyable and honest presentation and meets several other people who are involved in the business, all of whom strike him as friendly, positive and professional. He goes away to think about the opportunity, but his overriding impression is: 'I could certainly work with a team like that'.

John gives serious consideration to joining the business but decides against it because he enjoys his work and has some major goals which take up all his available time at present. He likes the products though, and becomes a customer. He really wants you to do well with the business, so what do you think happens when you ask: 'John, will you do me a favour? I'm sure you know some people who would appreciate looking at an opportunity like this – could you give me a few names?' John makes a real effort to help you out with some leads. Do you think he would let you contact his acquaintances unless he was absolutely certain that he could trust you to approach them with a positive and professional attitude?

With your new leads you have more chances to make a good impression in the same way, which will lead to even more chances, and so on. In the long run you are going to sign up a lot of people in this way. Just as importantly, you are going to leave a trail of good impressions about yourself, your company and everyone involved with it.

You can see how a positive and professional attitude can help you develop a potentially continuous flow of contacts from just one person on your contact list. But you have at least another 100 names on that list! Do you think you will ever run out of names?

We have not finished with John yet. He was happy to agree to you contacting him once a year to let him know how you were progressing. Twelve months later a note in your diary tells you to call him. He is pleased to hear how well things are going for you and explains how his circumstances have changed in the meantime. You suggest that he looks again at your business opportunity, especially as it has developed into an even better one over the past year with the benefit of experience and continued success. He does. This time he's ready for it and joins your team.

Suppose we are pessimistic and assume that John never joins your business. He nevertheless retains a high regard for network marketing done properly and will start to promote that view in any discussions he has on the subject. This could lead to him putting you in touch with further prospects. Your positive and professional attitude has maximised your effectiveness throughout this chain of events.

How your team will find your star performers for you

In the long run, the majority of people you sponsor will come from the third category previously mentioned – the people you will get to know and the people they will get to know. This is possibly the most exciting aspect of network marketing. It is not only you who is looking for the future stars of your business. They could be discovered by literally anyone in your network, and this is in fact more likely than you finding them all. Here is a typical real example.

Sally sponsored Linda, who soon became inactive in her business but not before sponsoring Gail. Gail was slightly more active, and her first recruit was Dinah, who became one of the company's top ten distributors. Dinah sponsored a business contact, Laura, who immediately sponsored an old friend, Jill. Jill became a top achiever in the business, and among her many recruits was Sue, who enjoys building her business slowly but surely. One of her first distributors was Phil, whose business is growing much faster than Sue's. Some time later, after developing a good-sized team, Phil sponsored an extremely active distributor, Sara, who is already looking like another top performer. This line of sponsorship (with high-performing distributors shown in bold type) now looks like this:

Sally → Linda → Gail → **Dinah** → Laura → **Jill** → Sue → **Phil** → **Sara**

Sally will receive bonuses on the group sales of Dinah, Jill, Phil and Sara, none of whom she found herself. Similarly, Dinah benefits from the team performance of Jill, Phil and Sara, whom she did not find herself. It would not be too disastrous for Sally and Dinah if Linda, Gail, Laura and Sue all became inactive. You can see from this example how important it is to work with your downline distributors to help them find their stars, who become yours too.

Developing a positive attitude

We have talked about 'a positive attitude', but you might well ask: 'What is it, how do I know if I have it, and how do I get it if I haven't already got it?' Many people are sceptical of even the phrase itself and will dismiss the whole subject as 'one of those American fads'.

Most people's experiences of life and work are very restricted. Most people earn a living by working for someone else. Their working hours tend to be controlled by others, as does the size of their incomes. They are used to strict routines and activities directed by others. This environment engenders a feeling of security even though the employer's decision could put an end to the job at any time.

What motivates an employee? What gets him or her out of bed in the morning, through the traffic and into the workplace at the same time every day? Ideally it would be love of the work, but we know that is often not the reason. In most cases the motivation is to keep the job, to avoid being sacked. They need the money, so they need the job, so they do whatever is necessary to keep it. That is negative motivation.

If you want to release the potential of network marketing, you will have to learn to step into the world of self-discipline, self-motivation and goal setting. However non-threatening this new environment is (and network marketing is probably the least traumatic way to move into business for the first time), there is a great deal to learn. Developing a positive attitude is perhaps the most important. It is a big challenge for anyone, but like any other great goal – making £1,000,000 through your network business, for instance – you can do it in small steps. The best way to start is by reading books, listening to tapes and attending as many business meetings as you can.

I had never thought that my own attitude was too bad; I still had plenty of friends when I was introduced to network marketing at the age of thirty-two! When I started going to the various meetings I was fascinated by the range of self-improvement and inspirational books and tapes available. After I had bought, read and listened to some of them I began to realise just how much room I had for improvement. The two books which had the most profound effect on me at that time were *How to Win Friends and Influence People* by Dale Carnegie and *The Magic of Thinking Big* by David Schwartz. I started to put into action many of the principles expounded in these books and found that they really did work.

Take, for example, the first part of the Dale Carnegie book: *Fundamental Techniques in Handling People*. The first principle is:

'Don't criticise, condemn or complain'

Think about that for a moment. How many times each day do you do one of the three? It was certainly in double figures for me. Gradually I drummed this rule into my head and found that it really did improve my relationships with people, especially those closest to me.

I'm still trying to improve, but this rule, amongst many other good ones to be found in that book, now guides all my relationships with people. Without a doubt it has greatly assisted the development of our network. Not only that, it has increased my enjoyment of life generally.

Consider two more of Carnegie's principles which are invaluable in this business: *'Become genuinely interested in other people'* and *'Arouse in the other person an eager want'*. The guidance in Carnegie's book is indispensable in developing the right attitudes for success in network marketing.

There are hundreds of books, audio and video cassettes, and even CD-ROMs covering this subject. You need only go to the relevant section of a good bookshop to see what is available. Better still, find out what is available through your upline and company. They will know from experience what items are most effective for network marketing. In more established companies you may also be able to purchase live recordings of seminars by very successful distributors, which of course will be specific to your particular business.

Read a few pages and listen to ten minutes of a tape each day. You will soon see where you can improve your thinking and your attitude. Put the advice into action. Try to make one small improvement each week. Within a year you will have developed 52 good new habits!

Probably the most useful action you can take right away to develop your attitude is to start associating with the people who are already at the level of business success that you aspire to. Ask them questions, notice how they handle themselves, examine their attitudes, and see what you can learn.

Professionalism

Think of people in the traditional professions – say medicine or law. You would expect a certain level and quality of service from any practitioner in these fields. Indeed, their own professional organisations demand such treatment of their clients, with a final sanction of expulsion. We consider that network marketing is a profession which demands similar high standards of conduct by its practitioners, the difference being that there is no central body to regulate this conduct.

In our view, professionalism in network marketing includes:

- Being businesslike and honest in all situations;
- Treating people as you would have them treat you, i.e. as intelligent and rational (at least until proved otherwise);
- Respecting people's views and decisions;
- Setting an example which, if followed, will ensure a fast-growing and profitable business.

A real example of unprofessional conduct will illustrate these points. This is one of many similar events which occur all too often. Ian and Sally received a telephone call from an acquaintance they had not seen or heard from for many years. The conversation went like this:

'How are you Ian? Long time no see. Look, I'm in your area tomorrow night, can I come and see you?'

'Sure, come round for a drink Steve, I'll look forward to it.'

When Steve arrived he had an unexpected and uninvited guest with him: his sponsor. Within ten minutes a whiteboard had been set up in the lounge and Steve's sponsor was giving Ian and Sally a presentation of the business opportunity. Ian and Sally were so surprised that they did not take in much of the information. They were embarrassed and felt that Steve had abused their friendship and hospitality.

What was wrong with Steve's approach? Quite simply it was unprofessional and therefore ineffective because it was deceitful. Ian and Sally might well have been interested in looking at a business if they had been asked in the right way. Steve should have treated them with respect as having enough intelligence to decide whether they were interested in seeing his presentation.

Quite unlike the story of John and Joe Smith, Ian and Sally will probably not want to see Steve again, let alone subject anyone else to the experience they had. It is also doubtful whether they will ever have a good word to say about the unfortunate company or products that Steve was working with, however good they happen to be, or about network marketing itself.

Unprofessional actions reduce the potential for long term success, professionalism expands that potential.

Goals

We will not cover the subject of goals in any detail. Goal setting and goal achievement is a major subject in itself and many excellent books are available. It is, however, important to say a little about the relevance of goals to attitude.

When you start something new, especially network marketing, you need to set some new goals which will stretch you. You will be taught how to set short, medium and long range goals. Whatever your real reason for getting into network marketing – your dream – you need to have a plan for achieving it. The big goals have to be broken down into smaller ones which can be achieved on a daily, weekly and monthly basis. When you have a plan to work to which will result in the fulfilment of your big goal you will notice how your attitude changes.

The achievement of each small goal on the way is motivating and confidence-building; you know you are getting there. Your self-esteem rises. People, especially in your team, notice the difference in you. It becomes easier to talk to people about the business and easier to sponsor. Your business moves even faster. Your improved attitude will duplicate throughout your team, making a positive contribution to everyone's attitude and to the growth and enjoyment of your business.

Confidence

The most powerful asset you can have in your business is total confidence in what you are doing. It will help you considerably in acquiring and developing the attitudes we have talked about above. If you are completely confident about every aspect of your business and where you are going with it you will become a powerful attractive force to others. Most people do not have much confidence in what they are doing and where they are going, so your own sense of purpose will help you to stand out from the crowd.

Total confidence will not come quickly, however. There are four areas in particular in which you will need to develop confidence:

- Your products
- Your company
- Network marketing
- You

Confidence in the first three areas comes from three sources:

- Facts
- Personal experiences
- Others' experiences

Facts. Learn all about the products you are dealing with, from company literature, published literature on similar products, and any reliable statistics. Get the facts on your company. What gives you confidence in them, and why? Know your industry well. Don't pretend that other network marketing companies do not exist, they do, so learn all about them. Get the facts and compare, know why your company is the best for you and one of the best in the industry. Read all you can about the business and make sure you are using your time as effectively as possible.

Personal experience. There is no better teacher than your own experience; no better confidence builder than your own satisfaction. Use the products and know why you think they are the best. Work the business and find out how the company treats you. Develop confidence that you and the company are working together for your future. Start building a team and experience the power of network marketing for yourself.

Others' experiences. Save time and energy by finding out what others did and thought; better to learn from their mistakes than make them again yourself. How do your associates get on with the products? What do your customers think of them? How do your associates rate their treatment from the company? Who in your upline has been in network marketing the longest, and what have they learnt? What do your non-distributor friends think about the concept, and why? What can you learn from this? One of the best reasons for going to training functions is to talk to and learn from others. The more successful they are, the more you will learn, so seek out the stars of your organisation.

Developing confidence in yourself can be the hardest job of all. There is no short cut, but you can ensure a continual increase in your own self-confidence with a constant diet of positive information. We recommend strongly the following activities as a good starting point: read the right books; associate with people who are where you want to be or going where you want to go; take action. Do what you know you need to do and improve each time. On a continuing basis it is important that you make full use of the 'tools' (books, tapes, videos and functions of all types) provided by your company and upline to help you and your business to develop.

Action agenda

1. Take some time out, every day, to develop your confidence, your attitude, yourself.

2. Always act professionally. Using the guidance in this chapter, write down around ten standards of professional behaviour which you would like to apply to your business. Review it every week: are you living up to the standards you have set yourself?

Chapter 8

The telephone – key to your success

Your telephone is the single most important piece of equipment in your network marketing business. Why? Because making phone calls is *the* most efficient way of contacting people. There is no other way to make as many effective contacts in a given period. You want £1,000,000 from your business as soon as possible? Get *good* on the phone, and get on the phone *often*. You can speak to people in person very effectively, but you have to be where they are. You can write, but that takes a lot of time and is usually a less powerful approach. You can advertise, but that is costly, time-consuming and unreliable.

This most important activity in network marketing is also the one that most aspiring networkers find the hardest to do. They will find any excuse not to do it. They will try all sorts of ways to get people interested in their business which do not involve the ordeal of picking up the phone. Advertising, mailshots, leaflet drops, posters – you name it, they will try it. Eventually, if they have not quit in frustration, they all come to the same conclusion: the phone is best. The telephone is so crucial that it is fair to say that your level of success in network marketing at any time is directly proportional to the number of times you have picked up the phone since you started your business. You will make hundreds, maybe thousands, of calls to prospective distributors in the course of a year. If you can make a 10% improvement in your efficiency (= doing things right) and effectiveness (= doing the right things) your annual income would improve significantly.

Now we can look at how to use the telephone properly.

Relax!

You are not asking for a £50,000 loan. You are not asking for their daughter's hand in marriage. You have no unpleasant news to tell them. So why are you nervous? It's because you want to get them to do something for you, right? You need them to help you build your business, yes? In this case your thinking is all wrong, so let's start again.

Put yourself in the shoes of some of your successful upline distributors who are doing really well with the business. Do you think they are grateful to their sponsors for being shown the business opportunity? Of course they are. Forget the idea that you are trying to *get* someone to do something for *you*, and turn your thinking around to what *you* can do for *them*.

Why are you involved anyway? You looked at an opportunity. It appealed to you. You checked out the company and satisfied yourself that it had a solid future. You were impressed by the products and felt you would be happy using and recommending them.

You found out about network marketing and satisfied yourself that it was a good, ethical way to do business. You met some of the people involved and felt that you could trust and work with them. You saw an exciting and profitable future for yourself. Think of that as you prepare to make your calls. That is what you have to offer. If your approach is right you will find that people are usually flattered that you have thought to call them. Few people object to being asked a couple of simple questions, provided they are asked in the right way.

Now you're thinking about the person you are going to call instead of yourself – a much better start!

The phone is for *contacting* not *explaining*

Always remember that the purpose of your call is *not* to explain the business but to make an appointment. Why? Well, it simply is not possible to fully explain the business over the phone.

To make a decision on something this important requires far more information than you could ever give verbally. A prospective distributor will need to see and use the products, examine their quality, study the available company literature, sales aids, training programmes, and attend at least one meeting. Probably the most powerful influence on prospective distributors is meeting the people who are already involved in the business. Everything else may look perfectly good, but often people will waver over their decision until they meet other people who are involved. If they go to a meeting and see and speak to other people like themselves who appear friendly, and are confident about the business, they are likely to make a positive decision in favour of joining. All this can take days, even weeks, so don't try to do the impossible by compressing all this into a phone call.

How, then, do you tell them what is on offer and what is involved without trying to explain the whole business over the phone? Simple. On offer is a business with tremendous potential. What it involves is a commitment of several hours a week for a reasonable period. Would they be interested in *looking* at an opportunity like that? It is important for them to know there is no obligation at this stage. You do not want a yes or no to the business, just a yes or no to looking at the business.

Four categories of people

We can place everyone on your contact list in one of four categories, each of which requires a slightly different approach for maximum effect:

- People you know well
- People you know
- People you know of
- People with network marketing experience

Before we discuss approaches to people in these categories it is important that, for efficiency and courtesy on every call, you:

1. Establish that you are speaking to the right person;

2. Introduce yourself;

3. Ask if this is a convenient time to speak to them for a minute or two.

People you know well

This will include your closest friends, family members and colleagues. You probably know them well enough to know whether your opportunity would appeal to them, but you need to show them what you are doing because they will want to help you. They are quite likely to become customers, and may be able to give you several ideas and referrals which will help you. In any case they will all trust you enough to look closely at your business simply because you have asked them to. If the business is not for them ask if they know anyone who might be interested. Anyway, as a matter of courtesy to those you know well you should give them a chance to see what you're up to and pass an opinion on it.

People you know

This will be a much larger category than the first, and it should grow daily if you make a point of meeting people every day and making a good impression on them. However, they do not know much about you and perhaps you only know a little about them. Before any call you need to know what it is that you are try-ing to achieve. The answer on the first call is always – to arrange an appointment. This might be a meeting with you at their house, attendance at a local hotel for a business presentation, coming to a smaller meeting at your house, or perhaps simply an agreement to watch a video or listen to a tape about the business. No one in their right mind is going to agree to give up their time for an appointment without knowing what they will be seeing and whether they want to see it. So you must establish with your call, in the simplest possible way, what is on offer and what is involved.

Even before you answer those two unspoken questions there is often another one which is useful to answer before it gets asked: 'Why me?' A fair question, and a good answer – an honest answer – makes for a powerful approach. Tell them the truth. You would not bother contacting someone you thought was an ignorant layabout. Hopefully you will contact only those people you think you can work with, and who appear to have qualities that would be beneficial in your business or whose circumstances are such that they might need your business. Here are some examples of how to start your call to people you know or know well:

> *'Bernard, I remember you saying you wanted to get out of your retailing business sooner rather than later. I've come across something that might help you.'*

> *'Richard, I noticed how well you get on with people who come into your shop.'*

> *'Chris, it's been a while since we last met, but I've been trying to think of some capable and reliable people who could help us develop our business in your area. You were the first person who came to mind.'*

You have not only suggested that they have the potential to succeed in your business but you have also complimented them. Now they are going to listen carefully. What you are doing is finding out what people need and offering them something that will fulfil that need. Sometimes they have already told you what they need at a previous encounter (e.g., Bernard, above) and this qualifies them as potentially interested in your business. At other times you designate them as being suitable candidates (Richard gets on well with people, Chris is capable and reliable) and then you have to find out if they have a need.

Ideally, you will get a straight answer to your question (i.e. would they like to look at an opportunity?). In practice it is normal for your prospect to want to know what kind of business this is. If you are evasive they may not take you seriously. There is nothing to hide, but, as we have explained, there is no point in trying to explain the whole thing at that point. What usually satisfies their curiosity while allowing them to keep an open mind is to describe the business in very general terms. For example:

> *'We're building a distribution network for an international company'* or;

> *'A major corporation is offering us the chance to help develop its U.K. market'* or;

> *'We're helping people set up their own businesses in... with back-up from one of the biggest companies in the field'* or even;

> *'It's a network marketing business, does that mean anything to you?'*

There are many things you can say which honestly explain the opportunity, without giving enough information on which to make a decision. You will do your prospect a disservice if you unsuccessfully attempt to explain it in full over the phone and lose their interest. It could have been the opportunity they really were looking for.

Some networkers advise that you should not mention your company's name during your first approach. This advice is based on the assumption that if the prospect has heard of the company he will have a preconceived opinion due to insufficient information and therefore will not agree to make an appointment.

In general we have found that the person you speak to will not have heard of your company. Its name will mean nothing to them, so it makes no difference whether or not you use it. If you do not mention the company's name, however, you may risk your precious time making a presentation to someone who has already examined your business opportunity thoroughly and decided against participating. The choice is entirely yours.

People you know of

In due course you will want to contact people in this category. These are people you know about, but who probably don't know you. For whatever reason you have decided that they might be interested in the business. It could be, say, a local shopkeeper, or one of a list of people referred to you by another prospect.

What is most successful here is to be brief and professional. Simply tell them how you know of them or how you (legitimately) got their name and number. Give them a good reason why you have chosen to call them and ask for a very low level of commitment, e.g. to listen to a tape, watch a video or meet you (and perhaps your sponsor too) for fifteen minutes. Your brevity and professional approach will build respect.

On occasion the authors have been contacted with a view to being sponsored by keen networkers from various companies. The most ineffective of these approaches have been have been those where the caller, after introducing himself, has proceeded to give a seemingly unending monologue on the features and benefits of his company, without any attempt to establish the listener's level of interest. Some networks are trained to use this type of approach because it is easily duplicated. In our case (and, we suspect, with many others) it is counter-productive.

People with network marketing experience

Some of what we have said above will not apply if you know that your prospect is familiar with the network marketing concept or has experience in the field. You can simply ask if they are still interested in network marketing as a vehicle for improving their situation. If not, why not? Aspects of your company's opportunity might overcome the objections they have. If they are still looking, they will be pleased to assess your business.

A word of warning here about approaching existing distributors of other network marketing companies. Direct Selling Association member companies agree to abide by a code of conduct which prohibits their distributors from approaching any other member company's distributors for sponsoring purposes. Also, it is generally considered unethical practice to 'poach' distributors from another network company. However, I like to think that most people have enough intelligence to make up their own minds about opportunities they come across and so cannot be poached against their will like a trout. I see nothing wrong in asking anyone in network marketing if they are happy with their company or products or progress. They are quite at liberty to say: 'yes thank you'. However, many people make one or two unsatisfactory choices before they find the right network business for them. People you know in network marketing should all go on your list. They will be interested in what you have to say – they have been in your shoes before!

When I wrote my prospect list I omitted a networker that I had been in contact with previously. Perhaps I had worried about 'poaching'. Six months later I met him at a business presentation. He was now with our company, doing extremely well – in another downline! Now I always work by and teach this rule:

If you don't ask them, someone else will!

Scripts

There are several schools of thought as to the best way to contact people by telephone. One method is to learn to say the same thing to everyone. That is very simple, but is it effective? Probably not, because everyone is different, and you will probably not come over as being sincere. It is all very well learning a script by rote, but what if you get a question that your standard phrases have no answer for? Of course, everything works if you do it enough times, but we hope to help you achieve a higher success rate by making each call as effective as possible. To do this you have to keep your mind on the people you are contacting and offer them the opportunity in terms to which they can relate. Of course, this takes a little more time and effort.

Although verbatim scripts may be ineffective, we have found that written prompts using bullet points and even individual short scripted sentences can be very useful. The way to do this is to develop your own phrases that you feel comfortable using, then add prompts relevant to the person you are contacting. In this way distributors who are not used to using the phone for business can develop an effective approach which includes all the important points, while still retaining their own unique personality.

Below is one example, to give you the flavour, but remember that everyone's approach will be different depending on the company, the products, the person being contacted, and so on.

Here, I am planning to talk to an old acquaintance from school days (25 years ago!) whom I met at a reunion a year ago, where we exchanged addresses and phone numbers. My prompts look like this:-

- How are you, etc.
- Something that might interest you
- Involved in fast-growing business – know the company?
- Looking for capable people in Essex to help us expand – thought of you
- Meeting/watch short video?
- Call again next week.

Above all, be yourself. Nothing is more credible and easy to learn.

Summary

Some people, and some books, say that you should not spend more than a minute on a call to a prospect, otherwise it will be ineffective. We say make it short but be relaxed and confident – be yourself. Inevitably you will make some small talk first with certain people. That is not a problem, but do make sure your prospect knows it is a quick business call. You will be taken much more seriously than if you slip in your invitation at the end of a long personal discussion.

To summarise what you have learnt about using the phone to approach people about your business:

1. Relax and get your attitude right – you have something great to offer.

2. Introduce yourself and speak to the right person. Is it convenient?

3. Are they interested in looking at a business opportunity a) with tremendous potential; and b) which requires only a minor time commitment initially?

4. Briefly describe the business if necessary, but don't go into detail.

5. Make an appointment.

Putting it all together

Here is an actual conversation I had with a prospect called Bernard. I had met him a year previously on a weekend course. Bernard and his wife had a village shop which they wanted to sell because it was not making a profit, even though they were putting nearly all their waking hours into it. Notice how all the five summary points above are included in the discussion.

'Bernard? Hello, it's Peter. We met last year on the course.'

'Hello Peter! It's good to hear from you, how are you?'

'Terrific, thanks. Can you spare a couple of minutes right now?'

'Sure.'

'So how about you, how's the shop going?'

'No better than it was, Peter, it's proving difficult to sell because we're still not making a decent profit.'

'Well, the reason I'm calling, Bernard, is that I might have something that'll interest you. I've recently started developing a really exciting new business with the backing of a large company. It's going really well and we could do with some more capable people in our team to help us expand it in your part of the world.'

'Sounds interesting. Go on.'

'The thing is, it's got massive potential but it's very flexible and doesn't need a lot of time to get it going. We're running some business presentations locally to explain how it all works, can I invite you and your wife to the next one?'

'Yes please. Thanks for thinking of me.'

'You're welcome. The meeting's at .... on ...., but what I'm going to do first is send you a video which

*will give you a good introduction to what it's all
about.'*

Bernard and his wife watched the video, attended a
meeting, and after a detailed discussion decided to join
the business.

Use your phone well – it's the best friend you have in
this business!

Action agenda

1. Getting good on the phone requires lots of practice,
   so start now. You may never get rid of the butter-
   flies, but you will get them flying in formation.

2. Make sure everyone you know knows what you are
   doing and is aware of the opportunity. If *you* don't
   ask them...

Chapter 9

Great answers to tough questions

As you will have gathered by now, network marketing is a very different proposition to employment or traditional forms of business. Understandably, you will be cautious. Many questions will be arising in your mind. Write them all down and get satisfactory answers from your prospective sponsor or upline distributors.

Certain questions are so important – and therefore so common – that we are going to answer them in this chapter. This will save you and your sponsor valuable time. Most of your other questions are likely to be concerned with the details of running your new business, details which are specific to the company and distributor group you are considering joining. For these questions your prospective sponsor is the best person to give you the answers.

Isn't this pyramid selling?

During the late 1960s and early 1970s several individuals and companies used the network concept to promote unethical schemes which attracted the attention of the media. The emphasis was on participants purchasing large quantities of products at high discounts with the intention of reselling in smaller quantities at a high profit to new participants. There was a distinct lack of attention paid to the most important aspect of any business's long term success – satisfying the end-user, the retail customer. This, of course, is quite different to how genuine network marketing companies operate. Here is a list of some of the activities associated with 'pyramid selling', which you will (hopefully) not recognise in a good network company today:

1. Poor quality (or non-existent!) products.

2. Large joining fees.

3. Coercion to obtain higher positions and discounts by buying large amounts of products without first obtaining customer orders for them.

4. No rights to refunds on unsold stock on resigning from the scheme.

5. No written contract between the company and the distributor.

6. No real concern with, or training for, retail selling.

7. No fixed wholesale or retail prices.

The real difficulty with the use of this well-worn phrase is that everyone who uses it understands it differently. Some are old enough to have read about or experienced the activities described above. Others are thinking of schemes where the profits are based on recruitment of other participants rather than product sales, generally known as 'money games'. Some people even include every genuine network marketing opportunity within their own definition of pyramid selling!

There are plenty of 'money games' around today. For a more detailed discussion of these schemes you may wish to read Appendix 3 of my book *Multi-level Marketing – A Practical Guide to Successful Network Selling*. At the time of writing the Government is reviewing all the legislation covering network-based schemes and have issued a consultation document which asks whether 'money games' should be made illegal.

To the reader we offer this advice: forget the phrase 'pyramid selling'. It is unhelpful and confusing. Virtually all organisations throughout the world – companies, charities, democracies, families – are hierarchies which are pyramidal (or, more accurately, triangular) in shape. Much more so, in fact, than a network marketing organisation. There is a significant difference between the two types of organisation.

The traditional company hierarchy has a fairly rigid structure, with a fixed number of positions available. New entrants who start at the bottom have to work their way up through the structure to get to the top. The speed with which this happens depends to a large extent on when and where positions in the structure become vacant.

On the other hand, the structure of the network organisation is continually changing. Any illustration can only show the situation at a particular instant. New entrants join the network at *any* point in a newly created position, albeit at the lowest level of the marketing plan. Regardless of where in the structure the new person has been placed, they now have the opportunity to develop their own organisation by creating new positions for new people 'below' themselves. They remain the head of their own organisation at all times and may promote themselves by expanding that organisation indefinitely. Every person creates their own 'top' position, and the number – and earning potential – of these top positions is unrestricted.

There are no ethical or legal grounds for the network marketing concept itself to cause you concern, what is important is how it is done. Make sure you are satisfied with the credentials, integrity and future prospects of the company. Ensure that the products have quality, value and a real market. Make sure you are going to get sufficient support and training from your sponsor and upline. And make sure you have the determination to make the business work for you. Get those things right and you will have an exciting future in network marketing.

When will it saturate?

This is an understandable concern because it is easy to calculate that if you sponsor two people a month and every new person does the same, the whole population of the U.K. will be involved within 17 months. It does not work quite like this; if it did you and everyone you know would already be involved.

People often have a fear that they will not find a market for their products if they happen to have come across a few people in their locality who are also distributors for the company that they are considering. Nothing could be further from the truth. We could discuss this point for several pages, but it is better if we state some facts for you to think about. Here are ten statements and questions. Give each one of them some thought and we think you will conclude that fear of saturation is unfounded.

1. No company with desirable products has ever run out of potential customers;

2. Around *55,000,000* people in the U.K. are *not* involved in network marketing;

3. Over *2,000* people are born every day in the U.K. – another 800,000 possible customers and distributors every year;

4. Everyone buys food every week from a retailer, yet J. Sainsbury keeps on opening new supermarkets which are always successful;

5. Most people have a T.V. but sales of televisions keep rising;

6. Each distributor needs only a few sales per week or per month to build a successful network;

7. Only a minority of distributors in any network are consistently active;

8. Can you imagine a situation where *everyone* has already seen your products?

9. Can you imagine a situation where there is *no one* left who wants to make some additional income?

10. Your network can spread throughout the U.K. and perhaps into many other countries as well.

Isn't it too late to make any real money at this?

This is a frequently asked question, and it stems from the misguided opinion that one has to join a network marketing company early in its life in order to have any chance of succeeding. The view may have some validity with, say, an obviously short-lived money scheme, but we do not define such schemes as network marketing.

So why does this view persist? One reason is that the principles of a good network commission structure are not often known or appreciated by someone inexperienced in the field. Here are some of the features of a typical marketing plan used by any successful company:

1. It rewards personal selling;

2. It rewards personal sponsoring only in proportion to the resulting increase in sales;

3. It rewards teaching and support of people in the downline only in proportion to the resulting increase in sales;

4. It requires consistent sales and sponsoring (and, indirectly, teaching) for you to qualify for bonuses on sales of your network;

5. It encourages distributors to work with their most committed downline distributors, regardless of who sponsored them.

You will meet many people whose perception of network marketing is along these lines: 'Those at the top of the pyramid rake off a commission from those lower down, and those at the bottom have no chance of making any money.' A little consideration of the points above will show that:

1. *Only* those who sell, sponsor and teach will make large profits;

2. Large profits are based *only* on sales generated by selling, sponsoring and teaching one's distributor network;

3. Success is not dependent upon where and when one is sponsored;

4. Everyone has the same opportunity to build a large organisation.

Here are some reasons why it is probably better to join a network later rather than sooner:

- More distributors in your upline to help you;
- More chance of the company surviving and thriving in the future;
- More experience means better training by the company and the distributors;
- More effective and professional sales and business aids available;
- Sponsoring is easier because you have proven success stories to tell.

All these benefits mean that you can get your business off to a faster and more productive start than those who joined in the earlier days. Of course, someone who did join then will be earning more than someone who joined later on and worked just as hard – but only because they have been working for longer. Those who got in at the start and did not work will not have made any money.

I don't have enough time

'I don't have enough time' is not a meaningful state-
ment. That there are 24 hours in a day is not a problem, simply a fact of life. The real question is: 'Do I
want to do this or not?'

Think of any time-consuming activity you have ever
done: night classes; reading a book; going shopping;
sleeping; watching TV; eating; or whatever. If you had
not done it you would have done something else
instead. Everything you do, you do because you decide
(consciously or not) that that activity is the most
important thing for you to do at that time. Time must
be found for whatever you decide to do, and this
means that other things have to be postponed or can-
celled.

Opportunities – choices – present themselves every
day. Whenever you are faced with one you must make
a decision, even if it is a decision to do nothing. Right
now you are faced with a decision as to whether or not
you will take up a network marketing business. By now
you will know what benefits are available to you if you
work the business seriously; you know they can be
substantial in many ways. The question is therefore
not: 'Do I have the time?' but: *'Are the benefits important enough to me to find the time to work to achieve
them?'*

How much time will I need?

No one can give you a precise figure. The time it will
take you to reach a certain position or income level
depends on many factors: how much training you

need; how well you manage your time; how effective you become; and how much travelling you do, to mention a few. There is a generally agreed minimum below which your business would probably fail to grow: this is around eight to ten hours per week. However, this does not all need to be in two hour chunks. The beauty of network marketing is that it is so flexible, able to be fitted in to all those spare minutes between everything else you do. If you are worried about the time commitment that you think might be necessary, look at the list below. It identifies just some of the many ways in which your own available time can be maximised and duplicated.

- Your sponsor can meet and speak to people on your behalf;
- Your sponsor will help you to support and train the people you sponsor *and* the people they sponsor;
- Other distributors in your upline will also help with the above tasks;
- The company will inform, train and motivate your team as a matter of course through newsletters, recognition, telephone support, corporate training, PR activities and conferences;
- You can invite your long-distance contacts to attend opportunity meetings in their locality without having to go yourself;
- People you sponsor will be building your business as they build theirs;
- You can build your business as you go about your normal daily activities. Wherever you meet or talk to people you can develop your business, whether you simply put their name on your contact list or actually invite them to look at the opportunity;

companies will have a range of sales and recruitment aids which can maximise your time investment. For example, a good video presentation of the business can allow you to show the opportunity to five separate people in one evening while you are doing something else.

At this point we would like to refer you back to Chapter 3, where we discussed how you are able to duplicate your time by network marketing. Consider that point again.

The most exciting aspect of network marketing is the opportunity to multiply your available time. Assume that you can only find eight hours a week to invest in your network business. If you use the time effectively you should be able to contact 20 people, get five or six of them together at your home or office for an hour's presentation by your sponsor, and sign up one or two of them into the business; all in the first week.

Even if your new people also have only eight hours a week available, you have now doubled or trebled the amount of time that is going into the development of your business. If the three of you repeat the process in the second week you might find that a few of the new people have 20 hours a week to invest in their – and *your* – business.

By the end of the month the amount of time being invested in your business could be as much as 500 hours a week. Not bad when you consider that there are only 168 hours in a week!

Selling

'I can't see myself going out selling.'

If you have not already heard this, you will. Or are you thinking it now? Suppose you were offered a job as a marketing director of Proctor and Gamble, the giant household products company. Prestigious? You bet. Heading a massive international organisation... which sells soap, washing powder, etc. Not a great deal of difference, is there, between that and leading an international network of several thousand independent distributors?

The obstacle is caused by focusing on a small part of the picture – the sale of individual products – rather than on the big picture which is a massive organisation turning over millions of pounds worth of products every year. The real question behind it is much the same as we discussed earlier: 'How much do I want what this business can give me?' Enough not to worry about small beginnings and a few product sales each week?

What is selling, anyway? A sale is simply the exchange of goods or services for money (or other good or services). A sale takes place because one party wants, at a price he is prepared to pay, the product offered by the other party. The important word is 'wants'. A business can only prosper if enough people *want* the product at the price. It will not survive on any other basis. Of course there are plenty of salespeople around who are obnoxious, who will try to convince someone that they need something which they don't, who will try to mislead, coerce and cajole people into becoming unwilling customers. This happens both within and outside network marketing, but is far removed from

ᴊf selling you will have to do in your network
ᴊs.

ᴊᴄe a 'want' is established in the mind of a potential
customer the sale will take place naturally. You can
verify this from your own buying habits. How often
are you 'sold' something by someone? Is it not really
the case that you decide that you want something?
Your want might come from a need – you ran out of
washing powder and needed some more. It might
come from your own decision to purchase an item for
the first time – say a new hi-fi – in which case you will
go and seek out the product you want. Or it could be
that you saw an advertisement, a display, a demonstration, of something you did not even know you wanted
until you saw it and were inspired to buy it. This happens to me all the time when it comes to music, tech-
nology, cars, food and a thousand other things.

In all these examples, although a sale takes place, it
was you who **bought** the product rather than someone
having **sold** it to you. Probably 99% of all your spending is done in this way. If the product you wanted was
available direct from a reliable friend or acquaintance,
manufactured by a reputable company with an excellent guarantee and competitively priced, you would
not hesitate to purchase.

Here are some real-life examples of network selling:

***Ian** had some guests at his house for drinks. One of
them spilt red wine down her new white jumper. Ian
said: 'Come into the kitchen, I have something that
will shift that.' He treated the stain with a liquid
preparation and gave the woman a small sample of*

washing powder. *'Wash it with this and let me know how you get on,'* he said. *The following day she rang. 'Brilliant! Let me have one of each will you?'* She became a regular customer.

Alan met an old friend he had not seen for over a year, who commented: *'Hey Alan, you're looking great, you've lost weight.'* *'Certainly have'*, said Alan. *'I'm on this new nutritional weight loss programme.'* *'Tell me more,'* said his friend, *'I need to lose some inches myself.'* Three days and some free samples later Alan's friend was spending £30 a week on the programme.

Margaret loves jewellery. She wore quite a few items to work one day and said to her colleagues: *'What do you think of these?'* She left work that day with orders for jewellery worth £50.

John used his new mobile phone in the presence of a friend, who said: *'could really do with one of those in my business, where did you get it?'* A week later he had a new mobile phone and airtime contract, all arranged by John.

Ann said to her friend who worked in a large office: *'Would you take my catalogue into work and see if anyone would like to order any of the books?'* Her friend came back with orders worth £100 and chose £20 worth free for herself, for helping Ann get the sales.

These are all 'opportunistic' ways of generating sales from the social interactions which happen every day. In none of the examples could the distributors be considered 'pushy' or irritating to their friends and acquaintances, nor should the distributors have felt in any way that their activities were demeaning. The amount of turnover generated in this way should be quite sufficient to enable you to build a large and profitable network.

You might be thinking: 'Why does everyone have to sell if we can all just use the products ourselves?' Many have asked the same question and even within the best network marketing companies there are often distributor groups which promote personal consumption only ('don't sell, just use'). Here are a few of the reasons we disagree with that idea.

- There are many thousands of potential customers out there who want your product but who do not want to become distributors. The business is there to be had.
- Some of those customers will want to become distributors in due course.
- Every customer could refer you to several other people who may wish to become customers or distributors.
- In any network, the effect of each distributor seeking just a few new customers a month would be a many-fold increase in turnover and size of bonuses.
- This is a people business, and the more people you come into contact with the bigger your business will become.

How can I approach people confidently before I am successful?

You will inevitably be asked the question: 'So how well are you doing with the business?' We suggest that you answer honestly that you have only recently got started but you have certain goals which you have every intention of achieving. Quoting earnings of very successful distributors can be useful to prove what can' be done with the opportunity, but have no bearing upon what any other person can or will want to earn. However, if you can prove that other people can be successful, it does not need to be you setting the example.

You do not have to be earning a large income in order to be successful. You are being successful when you are working toward the goals that you have set yourself, i.e., when you start your business. If everyone waited until they were earning good money from their network business before they approached anyone, no one would ever get started. All you need is the confidence to know that you have successfully identified an enjoyable, ethical and potentially lucrative business opportunity which is worth a little of anyone's time to examine for themselves. When you are contacting people it is *the business* you are offering for their consideration, not *yourself*. Of course, if your prospect decides to join, he or she will have to be happy about working with you.

Having said that, however, it is helpful to have confirmation of what is possible with the business. This is where you can use the tools of the business to assist and reassure the prospective distributor. For example:

- Meetings and functions where you can introduce your prospects to successful upline distributors from various backgrounds.

- Video and audio presentations featuring a selection of distributors at different levels in the business.
- Company literature, particularly distributor magazines and newsletters where achievements of distributors are recognised.

As you achieve more in your business your confidence will grow naturally and it will become easier for you to answer people's questions with information gained from your own experience. In the meantime, use all the resources at your disposal – especially your upline – to help you.

Action agenda

1. Questions are opportunities. Seek them out, and lend this book to answer them. People will generally accept answers from an independent third party (the authors of this book!) more readily than from a potential sponsor.

2. Promise yourself that you will offer people the business without regard to your current level of success. What you think of your performance is not a good enough reason for withholding the opportunity.

Chapter 10

Conclusion

If you have read this book from beginning to end you have had the chance to study a lot of information that you would be unlikely to find elsewhere.

We have been as honest as possible about the reality of starting and building a good network marketing business. We have told you about the fantastic benefits available to you, but we have also prepared you for the potential difficulties and the possible unexpected challenges, something that is rarely done for prospective and new distributors. Our most fervent wish in writing this book is that you will have one of the following reactions.

We hope you will say: 'This is definitely the business for me. I now know what to expect and I'll be well prepared for it.'

Now you can get started knowing that there will not be any nasty surprises waiting around the corner. Your next move should be to contact your sponsor and arrange to implement the recommended start-up programme for your particular network. If you are not given a recommended reading list ask your sponsor what books are recommended by the company and your upline. Failing that, start with my first book

Multi-level Marketing – A Practical Guide to Successful Network Selling and follow on with some of the books listed in its Appendix 5. We know that a regular diet of positive information – on network marketing and self-improvement – will speed and strengthen your success.

Alternatively you might say: 'Network marketing is a fascinating business with tremendous potential. It's not quite right for me just now but I would recommend anyone to take a close look.' Perhaps it is not for you because you prefer to work alone, or perhaps you have everything you want right now. If this is you then we would simply ask you to remember the concept if you ever find that you need another string to your bow to provide yourself with extra income. Network marketing could be the perfect extra string, one of the few businesses that can be built up around whatever you currently do without any major upheavals.

In any case, may we ask a favour? The person who prompted you to read this book is working hard to build a better life. Before you get back to them please take a little time to think about anyone you know who could benefit by taking a look at this business or the products. Making a few referrals will not only help your networker friend but it could be the start of an exciting and profitable new venture for some of your friends and acquaintances.

There is a possibility that you are thinking: 'I would really love to make a success of a business like this, but I just don't know if I've got what it takes.' Take our advice on this, we know that *most* successful networkers felt this way when they started. You actually *do* have what it takes. The question is whether you *use* what you have. The support system of a good upline in a good company will help you to recognise what personal resources you have and to learn how to use them effectively. Because of the very low risk factor in network marketing it is a business that you can try out to see if you like it. So our advice is to try it, as there is very little to lose and a whole new life to gain.

Taking action

Nothing will happen unless you act, unless you *do* something. Like everything else you have learnt in life, you will not get everything right first time. You will get a lot more things right if you take advice from your successful upline and this book, and act on it. But you will still have to go through some personal trial and error. As you get more experience and knowledge behind you, you will become more effective at what you do, but until then you should learn from your own and others' experiences.

We have seen so many people come into network marketing and get nowhere. Those who set and achieve worthwhile goals are in the minority. Here are just three of the many reasons why people fail to build a business; make sure you don't join them:

Paralysis of analysis. Proper consideration of a venture that will consume your valuable time is wholly necessary. However, excessively detailed investigations into the minutiae of marketing plans, bonus payout statistics and other details will soon become a far less productive use of time than actually getting started with the business. If other people are succeeding in the business then so can you. Once you have established the quality and integrity of the company, the products and your upline the major factor which will affect your success is whether or not you get into action.

Disappointments. It has to be understood that not everyone will be as enthusiastic about what we are doing as we are! There are plenty of people around who will be negative and critical, perhaps some of the people closest to you. Don't get disappointed by individual setbacks – this business is about repetition. When you do the right things often enough the business works.

Refusal to learn. Those who want to do things their own way rarely achieve great success in this business. Effective network marketing always requires help and support based on accumulated experience. If there were short cuts to network marketing success they would have been discovered years ago and everyone would be using them. Learn from those who have reached the positions you want to reach; they have every reason to give you the best possible advice.

We want you to succeed in whatever you decide to do. If that means leaving aside network marketing for the time being, that's fine. We hope you will reconsider the opportunity later if your circumstances change. If you decide to take advantage of this exciting business opportunity now, you have already learnt more than most new distributors simply by reading this book. Keep up the momentum by doing the following simple but powerful activities – **NOW**:

1. Start compiling your contact list.

2. Liaise with your sponsor to put some dates in your diary for your first meetings.

3. With your sponsor, plan who you are going to contact first, and how.

4. Use your enthusiasm; let everyone know why you are excited.

We celebrate your success!

An invitation from the authors

We are keen to hear about how you get on with the ideas in this book. Please write to us and let us know:

- What you found most useful and how it helped you
- If there was anything you thought could be improved
- What you would like to see in future books.

If we use your ideas you will receive a full acknowledgement in future editions.

Please write to:

Peter Clothier and Trevor Lowe
Insight Publishing
Serendipity House
Greytree Road
Ross-on-Wye
Herefordshire
HR9 7DQ

Group leader?
Book distributor?

We can supply this book at quantity discounts.

For further details, ring the Insight orderline on:

01989-566600

Here is the *new* solution
to all your training needs!

Outstanding new materials

At last! A full range of quality **British** materials. to help you:

• Inspire your contacts about network marketing

• Give the best possible start to your new distributors

• Develop high-level leadership skills

• Improve motivation and goal-setting.

Don't miss out on the biggest training development in years. Just ring and ask for details of our full range of exciting professional materials.

Mail-Order Book and Tape Service

Looking for the very best in training and motivational materials from around the world? If you have any difficulty in purchasing what you need through your network, the Insight mail order service will be delighted to help!

Volume Supplies

If you are a book distributor or group leader, contact us for details of our discount book service. We can supply all titles in the Insight Network Marketing Library, together with a selected range of the very best training and motivational materials. And if you are thinking of setting up a new book service within your company, we can offer you **free** training and advice.

Training Consultancy

Why not get the top trainers in Europe working for **you**? Our new duplicatable Success System is already getting rave evaluations from some of the most experienced upline leaders in the UK. Learn the new training techniques that really make a difference. Cut drop-out rates and watch your business take off!

This service really is something special – it's going to take the industry by storm. And it's much more affordable than you think. For the best investment you can make in your business, contact us today for information!

Contact us NOW for full information about these exciting new services and we will send you:

- **A FREE catalogue and newsletter.**
- **A valuable bonus report**

Just ring our orderline on:

01989-566600

for fast and friendly service.

Or fill in the postal order form overleaf $\rightarrow$

Yes!

Please send me regular news about new publications and training services from the Insight Network Marketing Library.

Please send me my FREE catalogue and newsletter, plus bonus report.

Name _____

_____

Address _____

_____

_____

Postcode _____

Your Network Marketing Company

_____

Please mail to:

Insight Publishing
Serendipity House
Greytree Road
Ross-on-Wye
Herefordshire HR9 7DQ

pc1